The Psychodynamic Counselling Primer

Mavis Klein

PCCS BOOKS
Monmouth

First published in 2006

PCCS Books Ltd
Wyastone Business Park
Wyastone Leys
Monmouth
NP25 3SR
UK
Tel +44 (0)1600 891 509
www.pccs-books.co.uk

The Psychodynamic Counselling Primer

A CIP catalogue record for this book is available from the
British Library

ISBN-13 978 1 898059 85 1

Cover design by Old Dog Graphics
Printed by Imprint Digital, Exeter

CONTENTS

SERIES INTRODUCTION   1

INTRODUCTION   6

Chapter 1   **THE ORIGINS OF PSYCHODYNAMIC COUNSELLING**   10

Chapter 2   **BASIC ASSUMPTIONS**   15

Chapter 3   **THE STRUCTURE AND FUNCTIONS OF THE MIND**   22

Chapter 4   **HEALTH AND PATHOLOGY**   31

Chapter 5   **THE DEVELOPMENT OF PERSONALITY AND CHARACTER**   36

Chapter 6   **LATENCY, PUBERTY, ADOLESCENCE AND BEYOND**   47

Chapter 7   **THEORIES AND THERAPIES**   56

Chapter 8   **TRANSACTIONAL ANALYSIS—PSYCHOANALYSIS MADE CONSCIOUS**   69

Chapter 9   **THE PROCESS OF THERAPY**   93

Chapter 10 **PSYCHODYNAMIC COUNSELLING TRANSCRIPTS**   98

Chapter 11 **PSYCHODYNAMIC RESEARCH AND APPLICATIONS**   109

Appendix   **RESOURCES FOR LEARNING**   113

GLOSSARY   115

INDEX   120

ACKNOWLEDGEMENTS

Thank you to the many people who, over the past 30 years, have trusted me with their realities and have so enabled me to enlarge my own. And thank you to Pete Sanders and Sandy Green who, most recently, have so insightfully, respectfully and meticulously edited and designed this book.

SERIES INTRODUCTION

PETE SANDERS

COUNSELLING

Each of the Primer Series authors will of course have their own particular vantage point from which to view the field of counselling. Before you look in more detail at psychodynamic approaches, I think that it might be helpful to take a look at some definitions of counselling itself. It is particularly noteworthy that Mavis Klein, along with many others, takes the view that counselling is a QUALITATIVELY and QUANTITATIVELY different activity from psychotherapy (you will find this in her introduction to the book, pp. 8–9). She asserts that psychodynamic approaches are better suited to deeper exploration, and so we discover the tip of an iceberg of debates as we try to define different types of helping activity. If you do not find debate and respectful disagreement helpful, exciting even, you will find studying counselling difficult.

It is, therefore, important to locate the helping activity of counselling in relation to other helping activities at least in order to avoid confusion regarding the purpose of this book. This book is specifically aimed at people wanting to learn about psychodynamic counselling with little previous experience or knowledge of counselling or psychology. The key word here is counselling.

So what do we mean by counselling?

What is counselling for?
One way of defining counselling is to look at what it is useful for. In the past thirty years, counselling has become ubiquitous, and it is perilously close to being presented as a panacea for just about everything. Some critics say that the emerging 'profession' of counselling has much to gain for claiming, on behalf of counsellors and therapists, that counselling is good for everything. It would

be wrong to make such claims: counselling has its limits and part of being a counsellor is to know what those limits are. The problem is that when we are in distress, it is comforting to think that there is a simple answer around the corner.

The situation is not made any easier when we understand that simply sitting down and taking time out from a busy life can make things seem better. Counsellors must be able to explain to their clients the differences between this very important relief and comfort that can be gained from compassionate human contact on the one hand, and counselling as a specialist activity on the other. Counselling can help people in certain states of distress and usually involves change:

- change in the way the client sees things or themselves
- change in the way a client thinks about things or themselves
- change in the way a client feels about things or themselves
- change in the way a client behaves

Although many people will not be able to put it neatly into a few words, what they seek from counselling can be roughly summarised in a few categories:

- support
- recovery
- problem-solving
- gaining insight or self-awareness
- developing new strategies for living

The sort of distress that counselling can help is often called 'emotional' or 'psychological' and can include:

- stress—a very general and possibly over-used term, but there are some situations in life, especially those that you can't control, that might leave you feeling so stressed that it interferes with your everyday life
- conflict—at home or work
- bereavement—whether a relative or friend. Indeed, having anything permanently taken away might lead to a feeling of bereavement, such as losing your job or losing your ability to do something like walk, play sport or have sex

- depression—another over-used term and not one to be taken
  lightly. Many life events can make us feel low, and talking it
  over really does help. The popular term 'depression' can
  cover everything from feeling understandably low after
  having your purse stolen or losing your job, through to
  being unable to get up in the morning or eat properly
  because you think life is not worth living
- coping with poor health, e.g. having a long-standing health
  problem or receiving a diagnosis of a serious or terminal
  illness
- trauma, e.g. surviving (including witnessing) something
  very disturbing (including abuse of various forms)

What counselling is not for

When someone decides to attend counselling sessions, they are,
by definition, distressed. It is, therefore, particularly important
that the client doesn't have either their time wasted or their distress
increased by attending something that we might reasonably predict
would be of no help.

As we have already seen, it is difficult to honestly predict
whether counselling will definitely help in a particular circumstance.
Nevertheless there are times when counselling is clearly not the
first or only appropriate INTERVENTION. It is doubly difficult to appear
to turn someone away when they arrive because sometimes:

- part of their distress might be that they have difficulty
  feeling understood and valued
- they may lack self-confidence and a rejection would
  damage it even more
- they have been to other types of helper and they think that
  counselling is their last hope
- they are so desperate they might consider suicide

However difficult it might be, we have to be completely honest
with clients if we think counselling is not going to help. It would
be wrong to let them find out after a number of sessions, after
which they might feel that they are to blame for not trying hard
enough. The use of counselling should be questioned if it is likely

that their symptoms of distress are caused by:
- poor housing or homelessness
- poverty
- lack of opportunity due to discrimination or oppression

Problems of this nature are best addressed by social action. The counsellor as a citizen shares responsibility with all other members of society to remove these blocks to peoples' physical and psychological well-being.

It would be convenient if we could divide problems up into two neat categories; those of psychological origin (and amenable to counselling) and those of non-psychological origin (and therefore not amenable to counselling). However, there are some other causes of distress which, although they will not be *solved* by counselling, will undoubtedly be helped by counselling in that the person concerned will be able to function better with the kind of support that counselling can provide. It may also be that the client experiences repetitive patterns of self-defeating thoughts and behaviour which renders them less effective in dealing with problems which do not have a psychological origin. It might also be that a person would be better able to challenge an oppressive system if they felt personally empowered, and counselling can sometimes achieve this. Such problems include those caused by:
- poor health (a physical illness or ORGANIC CONDITION)
- oppression and discrimination, including bullying
- living in an abusive relationship

Counsellors must be constantly vigilant to ensure that their work with a particular client or clients in general is not contributing to disadvantage, abuse and oppression by rendering people more acceptant of poor conditions, whether at work or at home.

> Psychologists must join with persons who reject racism, sexism, colonialism and exploitation and must find ways to redistribute social power and to increase social justice. PRIMARY PREVENTION RESEARCH inevitably will make clear the relationship between social pathology and psychopathology and then will work to change social and political structures in the interests of social justice. It is as simple

and as difficult as that! (Albee, 1996: 1131, cited in Davies & Burdett, 2004: 279)

What is 'personal growth'?

Counselling in the UK has become associated with what might be called the 'personal growth industry'. Self-improvement has been a feature of our society for a hundred years or more and includes such initiatives as the Workers' Education Association supporting the educational needs of working men and women. More recently further education has embraced more non-vocational courses and reflects the fact that as we get more affluent we have to attend less to the business of mere survival. We can turn our attention to getting more out of life and along with other self-development activities, improving our psychological well-being proves to be a popular choice. Furthermore, when people have a good experience as a client, they sometimes see that learning to be a counsellor could be a further step in self-improvement.

This 'personal growth' use of counselling contrasts with counselling as a treatment for more acute forms of psychological distress as listed on pages 2 and 3 above. It is, however, no less worthy or ultimately useful. Fulfilled, happy citizens, able to put good helping skills back into their communities are an asset, not a handicap.

USING THE GLOSSARY

Words set in SMALL CAPITALS indicates that the glossary on page 115 carries a brief definition and explanation of the term. The SMALL CAPITALS can appear anywhere in the texts, quotes, subtitles or index, although a few terms are defined in the text *and* appear in the glossary. Where this is the case, they are not set in SMALL CAPITALS immediately adjacent to the definition in the text.

REFERENCES/FURTHER READING

Davies, N & Burdett, J (2002) Preventing 'schizophrenia': Creating the conditions for saner societies. In J Read, LR Mosher & RP Bentall (eds) *Models of Madness: Psychological, social and biological approaches to schizophrenia.* London: Routledge, pp 271–82.

INTRODUCTION TO THIS BOOK

To have read the title and picked up this book implies your acceptance of—or at least interest in—two presumptions. 'Counselling' implies that there are freely chosen INTERVENTIONS that can cure, or at least relieve, the psychological pains that beset human beings chronically or transitorily. And 'psychodynamic' refers to those forms of counselling which assume the existence and power of the unconscious mind and concern themselves with the elucidation of motives through the dynamic interaction between counsellor and client.

The dynamic point of view sees *conflict* within an individual's psyche as not only at the root of the dis-eases that prompt them to seek help but as inherent in every person's normal efforts to cope with life. Psychodynamic counselling helps people to resolve their conflicts essentially through perceptual change, which in itself can greatly alleviate symptoms and suffering as well as leading the individual to new productive and fulfilling action.

People who seek counselling do so to alleviate the psychological pains and symptoms of chronic conditions in their psyches and/or in reaction to current stresses in their lives, including such occurrences as bereavement, poverty, job loss, and unhappy relationships. In cases of clearly reactive stress, time-limited counselling may suffice, but for chronic conditions, requiring as they do the breaking down of the individual's resistance to change (see p. 94) and developing radically new strategies towards coping with life-as-a-whole, open-ended counselling is often justified. But even in response to transitory, reactive pain the psychodynamic point of view sees the unspoken request of the client as, 'Make me better without my having to change'.

Elucidating the changes people need to make to cure them of their psychological pains involves discovering the *meanings* of their symptoms. Revelation is the goal and the process is as much art as science. Accuracy rather than precision is the target, since QUALITATIVE as well as QUANTITATIVE truths can be accurate, whereas precision refers to measurable exactitude—which is irrelevant to subjective reality. Scientific research demands that findings can only be affirmed by repeated experimentation, so psychodynamic theories and therapies cannot be scientific because each human being's experiences are unique.

At every moment of our lives our overall response to our situation and to other people is informed by three contexts: the unchanging attributes of our humanity; our individuality; and our present stage of development. The relative influence of each of these contexts at a given moment may vary although, broadly speaking, our 'stage of development' tends to predominate in childhood, our individuality in our middle years, and, ideally, as we grow old, it is the spirituality associated with our humanity, especially in coming to terms with ageing and death, which prevails.

In our humanity we are all the same and united in our lifelong concerns with pain and death, good versus evil, conflicting quests for excitement and security, and the overall quest for meaning in our lives. These are constant dynamic components of our minds that counsellors and therapists need to be implicitly aware of as constants in every consideration of any human being.

Physically and psychologically our completed selves are products of nature and nurture. Nurture has its say—witness the increased height of recent generations and our increased longevity due to improved nutrition and hygiene—but today, the power of nature is seen to be dominant and is now precisely mapped. So how can we justify the deeply embedded presumption of all HUMANISTIC therapies that our personalities and CHARACTERS are etched out of the contingent experiences of our infancy and early childhood?

My own resolution of this problem is that our genetic predispositions probably determine—at least to a large extent—which experiences we remember as significant. We then *interpret* these remembered experiences as if they were *causes* of what we later become. But it doesn't matter that the environmental events of our early years may not 'really' be the causes of what we become but are selectively remembered by us in accordance with our genetic predispositions, which, in turn, may be in accordance with an even deeper cause, to Karma or whatever ... until we stop and call the 'final cause' God—or UNIFIED FIELD THEORY. Our perceived causes of our pains are the outcome of our natural need to PROJECT blame for our pains, to which we are entitled, with the proviso that, healthily, we equally accept the other side of the coin of our chosen currency; our own responsibility and guilt.

Notwithstanding the overwhelming power of our genes in determining our nature, we do have free will which is contained in the responses we choose to make to our own natures and to what befalls us. Our responses are our choices, and these have consequences. We cannot avoid making choices. Passivity is the self-delusion of 'no choice', but of course it is a choice and, like all other choices, has consequences. However constrained we are by the genetic hand we have been dealt and its complicit endorsement by our earliest childhood experiences, our free will is exercised on the long continuum between making the most and the best or the worst and the least of that hand. And notwithstanding that throughout our lives we are also tightly constrained to respond in accordance with our earliest conditioning, we have some wriggling room within our chains and our cages—which, experientially, can make a lot of difference.

In today's world, short-term therapy is the norm and the term 'therapy' is increasingly renounced in favour of 'counselling'. As well as representing the true state of affairs, I believe this change of terminology is also a manifestation of political correctness in which the idea of 'therapy' smacks of elitism and implies an unacceptably patronizing attitude towards the client. But all practitioners need to be aware that there is a true distinction between counselling and therapy that should not be blurred.

Counselling accepts the client's presenting problems at face value; and while it may touch on deeper, underlying issues in the psyche, it rarely insists on ignoring the manifest problems in favour of the deeper issues of which the manifest problems are symptomatic. To this extent, 'psychodynamic counselling' is something of an oxymoron.

True psychotherapy probes and pummels at the deepest levels of the psyche and involves the creation of a complexly intimate relationship between the client and the therapist. Counselling is more pragmatic, has a more ad hoc nature, and is easier and pleasanter for both practitioner and client than full-blooded psychotherapy.

I bow to current usage and will use 'counselling' and 'psychotherapy' interchangeably in my exposition in this book, but I ask the reader to bear in mind that, in practice, there is a distinction between them that deserves not to be overlooked.

RECOMMENDED READING

Brussel, JA (1961) *The Layman's Guide to Psychiatry*. New York: Barnes and Noble.

1

THE ORIGINS OF
PSYCHODYNAMIC COUNSELLING

All psychodynamic theories and therapies have their origin in and rest on the foundation of psychoanalysis, created by Sigmund Freud (1856–1939). Notwithstanding the professional critics and detractors of psychoanalysis, all would concede that many of its concepts have so seamlessly permeated Western culture as to be taken-for-granted assumptions even by people who have never heard of Freud. Consensual opinion deems Freud to have been one of the greatest thinkers of the twentieth century, and possibly of all time.

Received wisdom has it that Copernicus taught us that we are not at the centre of the universe; Darwin taught us that we are not special among species; and Freud capped it all by telling us we don't even know our own minds. So, to the extent that we have presumed God to be in our image, God was toppled along with Man, and more people than ever before presume him dead. Freud himself was a passionate atheist, avowing that religion was the expression of mankind's NEUROTIC unwillingness to renounce our illusion that there is a better fate in store for us than the realities of suffering, death and nothingness. He claimed that we find in God the features belonging to the omnipotent, benevolent father, whom we have healthily renounced individually by the age of about six.

Freud was born on May 6 1856 in a small town, Freiberg, in Moravia, but lived nearly all of his life in Vienna. He escaped Nazi persecution and came to England with his family in 1938 where he lived the last year of his life. The house in Hampstead, London where he lived is now the Freud Museum. Freud's daughter, Anna, founded a child psychoanalysis clinic in Hampstead and worked there until her death in 1982. Freud's grandson, Lucien Freud (born 1922) is reputed to be Britain's greatest living painter; and there is a striking likeness in Lucien's paintings of human beings in all the truth of their unadorned, raw vulnerability to the similar depiction of humankind by his grandfather, albeit in the different medium of words.

Freud was born into and began his career in the late nineteenth century when the prevailing culture contained a utopian vision of ideal human happiness promised by science. As a child of his time, Freud's first ambition and attempt was, with his background as a medical doctor, to construct and establish a 'scientific' psychology by applying to psychology the same principles of causality as were, in his time, considered valid in physics and chemistry, which he hoped would thereby achieve for his theory intellectual respectability. His first contribution was to neurology in the field of physical medicine, and he couched his earliest psychological formulations in neurological terms.

But the procedure he engaged in was not the scientific one of elucidating causes but the semantic one of making sense of them. In formulating his revolutionary idea that symptoms have meaning in the unconscious mind, and basing his treatment of patients on this hypothesis, Freud took the psychoanalytic study of NEUROSIS out of the world of science into the world of the humanities. It was not that Freud invented the unconscious mind—it had been present in literature long before his time, and formal psychotherapy had begun in the eighteenth century when treatment for emotional ills was taken over from the clergy by rationalistic medicine. Furthermore, Freud's near-contemporary, Friederich Nietzsche (1844–1900), (whom Freud often quotes) anticipated many of his ideas, but which Freud was the first to articulate in a systematic theoretical structure. Freud's revolutionary idea was that a symptom and its meaning is not the product of causes but the creation of a subjective mind.

The most significant transition in Freud's life was the death of his father in 1895, in reaction to which he began his lengthy and arduous self-analysis. His first use of the term 'psychoanalysis' was in March 1896. At the same time he began work on his magnum opus, *The Interpretation of Dreams*, which was published in 1900, but took eight years to sell the 600 copies of its first edition! Freud never wavered from his avowal in this work that 'the interpretation of dreams is the royal road to a knowledge of the unconscious activities of the mind' (p. 608). Repressed wishes or associations to them, he argued, are revived in our dreams whose images deputise for those wishes.

Early in his career he was interested in hypnosis as a cure for hysteria. This gave way to the practice he developed of 'FREE ASSOCIATION' in an effort to reveal unconscious emotions, and he increasingly emphasised sexual development as the basis of psychological tension. He believed that the symptoms of mental disorder are traceable to the influence of consciously taboo, and usually sexual, impulses which are repressed early in life and reassert themselves later as symptoms of dis-ease. When the repressed impulses are brought into the light of consciousness the symptoms vanish. But it was when he discovered the defences that block easy access to repressed material that psychoanalysis as a cogent theory and therapy truly began.

With his first ANALYSANDS Freud had open, friendly, and even sociable relationships, and most analyses were completed in a few weeks or months. It was only as the TRANSFERENCE (see Chapter 9, pp. 93–4) of unresolved issues arising in childhood revealed themselves as being PROJECTED by the patient onto the analyst that a more regulated and prolonged analysis was deemed necessary to effect a cure. Indeed, the resolution of the 'TRANSFERENCE relationship' became for many analysts the sine qua non of their professional practice. Thus the BLANK, po-faced PROJECTIVE SCREEN of the analyst was invented and became a de rigeur requirement of being a psychoanalyst, which, in orthodox psychoanalysis, has continued to the present day.

From the discovery of and growing emphasis on the centrality of the TRANSFERENCE relationship to psychoanalytic therapy, in the hands of subsequent generations of practitioners—as in all originally inspirational, creative movements—psychoanalysis became, as theory and therapy, increasingly bureaucratised and lengthy. Eventually, about forty years ago, it began to lose its credibility. Its practitioners became stultified in their rigidity of procedure, and those who submitted to it were largely limited to the self-indulgently NARCISSISTIC and rich who could afford the time and money to spend years in self-absorption.

But people continued to have psychological problems and the need of experts to help them solve them. Few in today's secular world are religiously observant enough to resort to seeking and accepting the traditional equivalent counsel of priests, rabbis or mullahs, so the profession of psychoanalysis has stayed alive, albeit in forms that have of necessity adapted to the spirit of our age.

The tripartite division of the mind into the superego, the ego and the id (for definitions and descriptions of the id, ego and supergo, see Chapter 2, pp. 16 & 19–20; Chapter 3, pp. 22–5) is the central component of Freud's understanding of mental structure. He emphasised the wholly unconscious functioning of the controlling and guilt-activating superego and its self-interested, anarchically impulsive opponent, the id. A large part of the ego, which mediates between the superego and the id, he also argued is unconscious, including its mechanisms of defence, leaving only a small portion of the ego assigned the fully rational consciousness in which we take such pride.

Apart from delineating the defences of the ego (which his daughter Anna later elaborated) Freud devoted most of his intellectual attention throughout his life to the warring relationship between the id and the superego. It was left to future generations to elaborate the structure and functions of the conscious ego, which has been achieved in various ways by the numerous post-Freudian psychodynamic theories and therapies. All these theories and therapies take, as given, all Freud's own discoveries.

Today people need and demand their problems be heard and dealt with quickly and relatively cheaply. Even in America where, until recently, health insurers accepted the long-term nature of psychoanalytic therapy and paid up accordingly, this is no longer the case. A few weeks or months is all that is allowed, and therapists are required regularly and frequently to justify the continuance of treatment for every patient. Expediency rules. Short-term therapeutic goals and procedures are the order of the day and the profession has rationalised and justified its adaptation in terms of 'EGO PSYCHOLOGY' that finds merit in dealing with the face-value level of people's problems rather than assuming that real cure can only be achieved by the lengthy process of accessing pre-verbal infantile memories. Nonetheless, psychoanalysis as theory informs virtually all forms of contemporary HUMANISTIC psychotherapy and counselling, continuing to bear witness to the genius of Freud.

RECOMMENDED READING

Freeman, L & Small, M (1960) *The Story of Psychoanalysis*. New York: Pocket Books Inc.

Freud, S (1979) *The Future of an Illusion*. London: The Hogarth Press.

Jones, E (1961) *The Life and Work of Sigmund Freud*. Harmondsworth: Penguin.

2

BASIC ASSUMPTIONS

THE MIND IS AN ENERGY SYSTEM

The mind is a reservoir of a fixed amount of psychic energy, which energy can be invested or withdrawn from ideas, objects and various functions of the living organism. The total amount of psychic energy in individuals may differ, but for each individual the amount is constant. Psychoanalysis (the theory of child development, pathology and therapy originated by Freud) is a THERMODYNAMIC MODEL of the mind, bearing witness to the nineteenth-century scientific materialist ZEITGEIST (spirit of the times) to which Freud was heir.

Notwithstanding that the energy of the mind is mobile, the aim of the mind as a whole is a HOMOEOSTATIC one, that is, to maintain itself in a constant state through its built-in tendency to keep psychological tension at a constant optimal level, similar to that which makes the body keep its blood-chemistry, temperature, etc. constant. For as long as we are alive, we are constantly swinging between arousal and quiescence. Permanent quiescence is found in death. It could be said that the closest we get to optimum blissful quietude is depicted in the image of an infant suckling or asleep at its mother's breast. And the closest we ever get again to this nirvana is in the brief quietude following sex in the arms of a beloved other. These are our glorious moments when arousal and quiescence, sex and death are reconciled in the *petit mort* of sexual orgasm. This is the ultimate achievement of the PLEASURE PRINCIPLE (see also Chapter 3, p. 22 and Chapter, 4 p. 31), the hedonistic aim of life, in the interest of which the psyche is aroused to a state of tension to find the satisfaction needed to reduce this tension and return again to quietude. The desire for pleasure and the avoidance of pain is the foundation of our biological nature, reflected in the mechanisms of our minds. Thus our bodies are in an excited state of tension when we are hungry, and are satisfied and relaxed after a good meal; we are tense and aroused when we feel angry, and return to quietude when that anger has been appropriately expressed. Paradoxically, the ultimate triumph of the PLEASURE PRINCIPLE is the reduction of tension to zero in the death of the organism.

TRIPARTITE DIVISION OF THE MIND

The mental mechanism which accounts for all of the thoughts, feelings and behaviour of human beings consists of the id, the ego, and the superego. At first, the mind is activated solely by the PLEASURE PRINCIPLE, contained in the energetic reservoir of the id, but is later modified by the REALITY PRINCIPLE, centred in the emerging ego, which leads the infant to replace hallucinatory wishes and their fulfilment with adaptive behaviour to the world as it is discovered to be. (The structure and functions of the id, ego and superego will be elaborated in Chapter 3.)

For example, from the newborn infant's behaviour, it seems she has no awareness of her dependence on anything or anybody outside herself for her impulses to be satisfied. But, at least by the end of her first year of life, she is very aware of her dependence on her mother, and she has learnt some adaptive strategies for manipulating her mother into giving her, rather than withholding from her, what she wants.

Seeing and wanting a toy on the top of a chest of drawers, a young infant seems to believe that his screaming desire will drop it into his arms, but by the time he is one year old he is likely realistically to climb on something to reach it.

The ego is helped to contain the unrealistic desires of the id through the action of the superego, or conscience, which recognises the restrictions and dictates of the outside world and distinguishes between 'right' and 'wrong' according to the standards of the social and religious environment in which the infant is reared.

If the original, primitive pleasure-seeking behaviour could find gratification unopposed it would do so, but the individual discovers that, without adaptation to the REALITY PRINCIPLE, pleasure pays the price of 'UNPLEASURE' (that is, pain) either as a consequence of punitive influences within its own mind or from punishments inflicted by the outside world.

INSTINCTS

MOTIVATION is primarily directed by the instincts, which seek fulfilment through the power of DRIVES.

According to classical psychoanalytic theory, an instinct has (a) a biological source (e.g. feeling cold or tired); (b) a supply of energy derived from that source (hunger or yawning); (c) an aim expressed through behaviour leading to the satisfaction of the instinct and discharge of energy (going to the supermarket or undressing); and (d) an object, in relation to which the aim can be achieved (buying some food or going to bed to sleep). All the energy for the work of the mind is obtained from the instincts. The impetus of an instinct is its strength or force, which is determined by the amount of energy it possesses.

The examples just given are experienced often by all of us in everyday life, but beyond these very simple examples, we also have sexual and aggressive instincts, which can sometimes be expressed directly, but are more often expressed in impulses derived from the instincts, rather than the instincts themselves (see 'defence mechanisms', Chapter 3, pp. 26–30). When the instincts are frustrated by their failure to find an object for their satisfaction, the outcome is an increase in tension, which is experienced as pain. This scenario of struggle to obtain pleasure through the expression of instinct is, according to Freud, what life is all about. The mind's reactions to instinct frustration will be elaborated in Chapter 4.

LIBIDO

Libido is the life force, which is the SEXUAL INSTINCT, conceived by Freud as congenital and expressed from birth even though the possibility of its mature manifestation in genital desire and sexual intercourse is not achieved until puberty. Before the age of three, libidinous energy is directed first towards the infant's own mouth in sucking and biting and then to its own anus and its products in defecation. The beginnings of libido directed towards the child's genitals occurs in the period between three and six years of age. (These stages of development will be described in Chapter 5.) Between the ages of six and twelve, sexuality is put on a back burner in favour of consolidating gender IDENTIFICATION and social skills. (This stage of development, and puberty and adolescence will be elaborated in Chapter 6.)

LIFE IS CONFLICT

Apart from hunger, LIBIDO as sexual energy, is understood to be the principle driving force behind all our interactions with other people throughout our lives, even though it is often bound to find indirect rather than direct expression, again see 'defence mechanisms', Chapter 3, pp. 26–30. But in some of his writings Freud postulated that LIBIDO is divided into the components of sexuality and aggression. On the one hand, this may refer to the aggressive component in the sexual DRIVE itself; but at other times Freud proposes that sex and aggression are opposed forces in the psyche, sex manifesting the life force and aggression the opposed self-destructive DEATH INSTINCT, which he called 'THANATOS'. Freud seemed never to quite make up his mind whether THANATOS actually exists, but its conceptualisation fits neatly into his overall perception that the instincts, in their primitive desire to express themselves, are always at war with opposed forces (from within the psyche or the external world) seeking to stop that expression.

When aggression is considered as a component, rather than an opponent, of sexuality, plausible examples can be found in sexual activity which includes wooing and submitting, forcefulness and tenderness, sadism and masochism, love and hate.

When aggression is considered as a manifestation of the DEATH INSTINCT, it may be justified biologically as death being the point to which the individual inexorably moves. That is, the final aim of any living thing is to reduce itself to the inorganic state from which it emerged.

HISTORY IS DESTINY

Psychoanalysis is basically historical, accounting for the development of adult CHARACTER by the challenging circumstances which the person experienced primarily between birth and about six years of age. It treats learning as cumulative, so that early experiences influence later experiences through our brain's hard-wired propensity to see the world, ourselves, and our relationships t0 the world and other people as constant. Having made our adaptations to the circumstances we experienced in the first six years of our lives, we *expect* these circumstances to occur repeatedly. And, out of our expectation, we unconsciously invoke similar experiences over and over again and make similar adaptations to them throughout the rest of our lives. This is a central assumption of psychoanalytic theory and is called the REPETITION COMPULSION.

Our resistance to perceiving our relationships to other people and the world other than by the perceptions we derived from the experiences of our first six years is a core component of psychoanalytic theory. This enduring theme returns in Chapter 6, p. 47 and Chapter 8, p. 70.

UNCONSCIOUS, PRE-CONSCIOUS, AND CONSCIOUS

The mental processes of the id and of the superego are unconscious and their aims can only be known inferentially. A considerable portion of the ego is also unconscious (see Figure 1, overleaf) specifically in the expression of its defence mechanisms.

The pre-conscious refers to the level of mental activity from which data, concepts, and experiences can be recalled readily. Such material is seldom associated with emotional conflict or the deeper DRIVES; it is the level of ordinary, everyday memory association. We are particularly aware of having a pre-conscious level in our minds when we struggle to bring into full consciousness names, words or ideas that are 'on the tip of our tongues'.

Full rational consciousness is contained in the ego, but is only a very small fraction of the overall functioning of the mind.

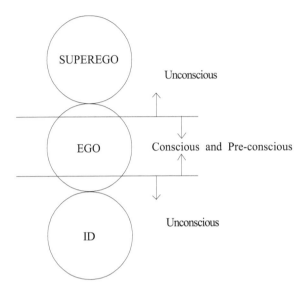

Figure 1   A diagrammatic representation of the psychoanalytic structure of the human mind

NATURE AND NURTURE

Although psychoanalysis talks as though the contingencies of our early childhood experiences are entirely responsible for our later personalities, CHARACTERS, and destiny, Freud never ceased to allow for the constitution of the individual person. That is, one individual might be frustrated by experiences that another can readily accept and accommodate to their desires. It is probably the case that CONSTITUTIONAL FACTORS determine which experiences in early childhood are noticed by the psyche and which dismissed as 'noise'. For there are a huge number of stimuli that bombard us at any time, but our brains are only capable of processing a very small fraction of that totality. Our minds then interpret those few remembered experiences as the causes of what we later become, even though our genetic predispositions may be the cause of our *selecting* the particular experiences to remember.

The clearest evidence of the way in which our brains seem to be biologically programmed to see characteristics in ourselves as being 'caused by' particular experiences is in the memories of siblings. Amongst grown-up brothers and sisters, some will remember childhood experiences they shared and others will claim no recollection of them; and even when they each remember the same shared experiences, their interpretations of the power and influence of those experiences can vary enormously.

RECOMMENDED READING

Hall, CS (1956) *A Primer of Freudian Psychology*. New York: Mentor.

3

THE STRUCTURE AND FUNCTIONS OF THE MIND

The division of the mind into the components of id, ego and superego is a core tenet of psychoanalytic theory. Whether or not there are anatomical structures in the brain corresponding to these components is open to question; but, functionally, their existence is an unquestioned principle.

Id

The id is the primary source of psychic energy and the seat of the instincts. The sole function of the id is to provide for the immediate discharge of excitation (energy or tension) that is released biologically by internal or external stimulation. This function of the id fulfils the PLEASURE PRINCIPLE, which is the primary aim of life. Tension is experienced as pain or discomfort, while relief from tension is experienced as pleasure or satisfaction. If all tension could be discharged there would be no need for any psychological development. But this is not the case. The first frustrations of impulse we experience are the release of the tension of hunger or the pain of indigestion, which inevitably are not always immediately gratified. And by the time we are grown up we acknowledge—even though we may not serenely accept—that frustration permeates our lives, from waiting for the kettle to boil to sexual longing for someone who rejects us.

The id lacks organisation as compared with the ego and the superego. The id does not change with the passage of time and cannot be modified by experience because it is not in contact with the external world. However, it can be controlled and regulated by the ego. There are only two possible issues for any id process. Either it discharges in action or wish fulfilment or it succumbs to the influence of the ego, in which case the energy becomes BOUND, that is, locked in place, instead of being immediately discharged.

The id is the world of subjective reality in which the pursuit of pleasure and the avoidance of pain are the only functions that count. The id is unorganised, emotional, volatile, chaotic, hallucinatory, lacking any sense of time, space or causality, utterly selfish. 'No' does not exist for the id, and there is no distinction between contraries; contraries exist side by side without cancelling each other out or diminishing each other. Our only access to the functioning of the id is through our dreams and, even then, only partially, because, as Freud puts it in *The Interpretation of Dreams*, 'a dream is a disguised [by the ego] fulfilment of a suppressed or repressed wish'.

Ego

In order to achieve maximum possible satisfaction, the id has to take into account external reality, which consists of the physical world and the constraints imposed by other people. This requires the formation of another system, the ego, which, in the well-adjusted person, is the executive of the personality, controlling and mediating between the id and the superego to maintain an optimum balance between the expression of impulse and its control. In contrast to the id's governance by the PLEASURE PRINCIPLE, the ego is governed by the REALITY PRINCIPLE. The ego is organised, the id is unorganised; the ego is mutable (changeable), the id is immutable.

Eventually, the REALITY PRINCIPLE leads to pleasure although a person may have to endure some discomfort while looking to reality.

The ego's function is called the SECONDARY PROCESS, in contrast to the PRIMARY PROCESS of the id. The SECONDARY PROCESS does not make the mistake, as the PRIMARY PROCESS does, of regarding the image of an object as though it were the object itself. It distinguishes between reality and fantasy. Although it is largely a product of interaction with the environment, its development is guided by natural growth processes leading to MATURATION. For example, talking usually begins at about one year of age and reading at about six years of age, although the acquisition of these (and other) age-related skills are, of course, also dependent on appropriate input from the environment.

As well as directing and containing the id instincts in accordance with the REALITY PRINCIPLE, the ego also has some functions which have ceased to be directly influenced by the instincts and are therefore not associated with conflict. In normally healthy individuals, speech, breathing and walking are examples of such functions. Any activities which have become functionally autonomous, such as reading and writing, are examples of successful ego development. (See SUBLIMATION, pp. 29–30 below.)

Superego

The superego is the third component of the mind—the moral and judicial branch. It represents the ideal rather than the real, and strives for perfection rather than for reality or pleasure. It develops out of the ego as a consequence of the child's assimilation of her parents' standards of what is good and virtuous and what is bad and sinful. By assimilating the moral authority of her parents, the child replaces their authority with her own inner authority, which enables her to control her behaviour in line with their wishes and, by so doing, to secure their approval and avoid their displeasure.

Like the id functions, superego functions are unconsciously performed but, unlike the id functions, are open to becoming preconscious and then conscious. Id functions are always executed unconsciously.

The superego is made up of two sub-systems, the EGO IDEAL and the conscience. The EGO IDEAL corresponds to the child's conceptions of what his parents consider to be morally good. In grown-up life, the EGO IDEAL often plays an important (albeit unconscious) role in our choice of people with whom we fall in love. Conscience, on the other hand, corresponds to the child's conceptions of what his parents feel is morally bad, and these are established through physical and/or psychological punishments. Approval by parents stands for love, disapproval is withdrawal of love, and these are connected to the satisfaction or frustration of his basic needs. For an infant even as young as about one year of age, a frown or a harsh tone of voice from mother can be experienced every bit as painfully as a physical slap. 'Does she still love me? Will she still look after me?' can be the excruciating bodily terror of infants long before they can articulate that terror in words.

A thought is the same as a deed in the eyes of the superego and, in this respect, it resembles the id, making no distinction between subjective and objective. The superego punishes the ego for thinking bad thoughts even though the thoughts may never be translated into an action. The psychological rewards and punishments employed by the superego are feelings of pride or of guilt or shame in the ego. Pride is equivalent to self-love and guilt or shame to self-hatred. Teachers, ministers of religion, policemen—anyone in a position of authority over the child—can reinforce or may elaborate the edicts of the superego given by the child's parents.

The ego is formed out of the id, and the superego is formed out of the ego. Once established, these three systems continue to counteract and blend with each other throughout life.

Civilisation

Basically, the superego serves the purpose of controlling and regulating those impulses whose expression would endanger the stability of society. These impulses are sex and aggression. The control of the id—and some of the ego—impulses by the superego is the foundation of civilisation, which the ego learns to value.

Civilisation is a pact our essentially selfish impulses make with other people. It is an agreement that effectively says, 'I will not harm you if you do not harm me. I will look after you and help you to survive when you are too young or too old or too handicapped or frail to survive without help, if you promise to do the same for me when I have such needs.' In particular, the REPRESSION of many of our sexual and aggressive impulses is the price to be paid for civilisation, and is the (mostly) willing compromise we make between our self-centredness and the self-centredness of others.

DEFENCE MECHANISMS

It is through the development of our egos that we learn to distinguish between self and not-self. Our sense of self is our sense of our uniqueness, and we hold this precept very dear. So an assault on the integrity of the ego creates pain of some kind, ranging from mild discomfort to acute anxiety. Anxiety in the ego may be instigated by attacks from instinctual tension (id), a bad conscience (superego), or realistic dangers (ego awareness of threats to our survival). When only a small amount of energy is invested in an impulse in the ego which is threatened with punishment, *suppression* of the impulse by conscious, voluntary inhibition may suffice to avert the danger, such as resisting another cream cake, or a client in therapy successfully deciding to give up smoking. But when the impulse is highly charged with libidinous energy, the unacceptable impulse must be REPRESSED (see Chapter 4, p. 35) and made unconscious by the use of defence mechanisms (see below for examples) in which some energy is invested by the ego to enable them to fulfil their protective function.

Once energised, the defence mechanisms constitute the irrational and unconscious part of the ego. They achieve a compromise between sustaining the ego's self-esteem and attacks upon that self-esteem. They act by distorting, hiding, or DENYING some aspect of reality, and tying up psychic energy which could be used for more effective ego activity. Nevertheless, within limits, they are a normal and healthy part of the ego, enabling it to function sanely in the face of all the challenges that inevitably beset it throughout life. Without ego defences we are insane. (See Chapters 4 and 9.)

Defence mechanisms may be actively defensive, aggressive, or compensatory, either dominantly one of these or involving combinations of the three. So, for example, a father of a teenage daughter may actively defend himself against incestuous impulses by avoiding seeing his daughter naked, and aggressively criticising the sexually alluring way in which she dresses. And a physically or psychologically abused child may avow and express excessive love towards his abusing parent as a compensation for the hatred he deeply feels for that parent.

The ego is victorious when its defensive measures enable it to restrict the development of anxiety and UNPLEASURE, and gain some measure of gratification, thereby establishing the most harmonious possible relationships between the id, the superego, and the forces of the outside world. It is the failure of the defence mechanisms that leads to NEUROSIS or PSYCHOSIS. (See Chapter 4, pp. 33–4.)

As the ego grows, the defence mechanisms available to it grow in sophistication and effectiveness. Below are listed and briefly defined the most popular defence mechanisms deployed by the ego.

Identification

According to Freud, identification 'is the original form of emotional tie with an object'. The infant at first completely identifies in his emotional life with his mother. Her demands are his desires. This defence is a valuable source of gratification throughout life, enabling us to lose ourselves happily in the stories of other selves who are the characters in books and plays and films we enjoy as well as in empathic understanding of intimate others. So, for example, somebody with repressed but very powerful aggressive impulses may greatly enjoy reading murder stories; and a sexually celibate person may immensely enjoy watching pornographic films.

Denial

Denial is the most primitive reaction of the emerging ego in response to threatened punishment from the superego for wrongdoing. It says, 'I didn't do it', when, to all the rest of the world, it did. Denial is telling lies to avoid punishment, which rarely works for very long. In grown-up life, it is observable, for example, in the alcoholic who denies that he has a problem, which is a last resort of his ego before its disintegration.

Projection

Projection attributes to another the ideas or impulses that belong to oneself. It gives what appears to be objective reality to that which is actually subjective, providing the individual with an excuse for expressing her real (usually negative) feelings. Projection is a very popular defence mechanism, because from a very early age children are encouraged to look for the causes of their behaviour in the external world and discouraged from examining and analysing their own motives.

(The writer of this book remembers, with amusement, primitively transparent displays of denial and projection in one of her granddaughters, then aged two. Standing in my kitchen with me, she dropped and broke a cup she was holding. Despite my completely non-punitive, 'Never mind' response, she compulsively and vehemently denounced the fact with, 'I didn't. I didn't.' A few weeks later, with an already more mature ego, sitting opposite me at the kitchen table, she accidentally dropped some food on the floor and, without batting an eyelid, stared at me and declared, 'I think you did that'!)

Displacement

Displacement is a variation of PROJECTION. Instead of blaming another person for its own inadequacies, the ego attaches blame to an object or idea. It is the 'bad-workman-always-blames-his-tools' syndrome. It is also involved in the 'dream work' of the ego, by which the ego protects itself from full knowledge of the id impulses represented by our dreams. Images in our dreams symbolise rather than directly express id impulses.

Some particular images in dreams are very commonplace and have well-validated general meanings; others are more idiosyncratic and may require unravelling by the individual dreamer. Dream subjects that usually have confident interpretations include *animals*, which are understood to represent 'animal instincts' in the dreamer; *snakes* represent sexuality; *caves* represent the unconscious mind; *clothes* represent the individual's thoughts and feelings that others expect of him, rather than those that are really his; *climbing* is a striving for success; a *bus journey* is about wanting to fit in with the rest of society rather than pursuing some private, personal aim; *departing* (from airports, stations, etc.) is about death; *money* stands for anything of equivalent value, often time or energy or sometimes love; *being paralysed* concerns conflicting impulses or emotions.

Rationalisation and justification

Rationalisation is the mechanism by which an acceptable explanation (not the true reason) is advanced for conduct. It is used to enable the individual to do or think what she wishes and then discover a good reason for so doing or thinking.

Justification is a form of rationalisation that makes a precept in the superego an excuse for doing or thinking what an impulse wants. A commonly accepted use of justification is contained in 'white lies', associated as they usually are with not hurting another person's feelings.

Reaction-formation

Reaction-formation occurs when one of the instincts produces anxiety in the ego and the ego tries to sidetrack the offensive impulse by concentrating on the opposite. For example, excessive love can mask hate. It is the excessive, exaggerated expression that is the key to defining it as a defence mechanism rather than an expression of authentic feeling. Reaction-formation is a highly energised and very strong defence.

Sublimation

Sublimation is considered by psychoanalysis to be the most positive of all the defence mechanisms. In it, repressed libidinous impulses are deprived of their specific erotic content and aim and are deflected towards new goals, non-sexual in nature and socially acceptable.

All sublimation depends on SYMBOLISATION, the capacity for which distinguishes human beings from other species. It is arguable that all the cultural artefacts of mankind—art, philosophy, science, literature, music, history, etc—are the outcome of sublimation. It might be said, for example, that an artist's occupation is about representing an EGO-IDEAL image of the world; a scientist is gratified in his work by the feeling of being in control of unpredictable and anarchic impulses of his id; a philosopher is hoping to find meaning in life; a musician may be seeking to overcome his ego problems by regressing to the oceanic feelings of his id.

While sublimation is singular amongst the defence mechanisms in its use of libidinous energy for purposes other than self-deception, it still contains some instinctual energy and aims as, for example, the NARCISSISTIC gratification associated with altruistic service to others and the aggressive, competitive impulse attached to intellectual or artistic achievement.

We all spend our lives swinging between DENIAL and sublimation and all the defences in between, in accordance with our developed personalities and CHARACTERS and in response to fluctuating and transitory challenges to our egos.

RECOMMENDED READING

Brenner, C (1957) *An Elementary Textbook of Psychoanalysis*. New York: Anchor Books

Chetwynd, T (1981) *Dictionary for Dreamers.* London: Granada.

Chetwynd, T (1982) *Dictionary of Symbols.* London: Granada.

Freud, A (1968) *The Ego and the Mechanisms of Defence*. London: The Hogarth Press.

Freud, S (1963) *Civilization and its Discontents*. London: The Hogarth Press.

Freud, S (1967) *The Interpretation of Dreams*. London: George Allen & Unwin.

4

HEALTH AND PATHOLOGY

In the mentally healthy person the three systems of id, ego and superego form a unified and harmonious organisation. By working together cooperatively they enable the individual to carry on efficient and satisfying transactions with her environment, thus fulfilling her basic needs and desires.

Biologically speaking, perfect mental health would be the immediate, unimpeded, energetic discharge of all the id impulses as they arise. In human beings this could only be achieved by ignoring the demands of the ego and superego, which would result in much UNPLEASURE through the punishments they invoke. So unadulterated mental health is impossible. The relative frustration of id impulses and biological dis-ease is the lot of being human. We are aroused, and we move, in response to our frustrations; the only lasting quietude is death.

Fixations

Human growth is a continuing evolution and gradual victory of each stage of development over the past. In the first six years of life the PLEASURE PRINCIPLE learns to achieve its optimum satisfaction while forming compromise adaptations, at first to the REALITY PRINCIPLE of the growing ego, and later to the taboos imposed on it by the superego.

As each stage of development progresses to the next, the id is BOUND, unwillingly, to relinquish more and more of its energy to the demands of the ego and superego. Healthy parents and caretakers of young children encourage these sacrifices with praise for becoming 'a big boy or girl' and explicit promises of rewards and privileges associated with 'growing up'. Nevertheless, each transition involves a further relinquishment of instinctual satisfaction for the child and rarely, if ever, achieves this without a struggle. Whatever privileges he is promised for moving on to the next stage of development, these are less real to him than the satisfactions he is being asked to surrender.

The normal process of moving from one stage to the next is, to a greater or lesser extent, only partially successful in terms of the child's transference of energy appropriate to the needs of the next stage of his development. Almost inevitably some energy remains invested in the earlier stage and is BOUND there. Such BOUND ENERGY is called a fixation.

Psychoanalysis proposes that there are three causes of fixations: (1) The child has not had sufficient appropriate satisfaction of its LIBIDINOUS needs at the stage it should be ready to leave. (For example, being weaned off the breast or bottle too early would cause an oral fixation.) (2) The child has been over-indulged at the stage it should be ready to leave (and being 'spoilt' has a diminished impulse to 'grow up'). (For example, being allowed to sleep between her parents until she is five years old would cause an Oedipal fixation—see pp. 42–6 for definition and description of Oedipal stage. By continuing to sleep between her parents at this stage she will illegitimately feel herself able to gratify her desire to believe that her father loves her more than he loves her mother. The boy who continues to sleep between his parents at this stage of his development will have a similar, gender-complementary experience.) (3) Gratification of the stage the child should be ready to leave has been intermittent or ambiguous, making the learning associated with that stage insecurely incomplete. (For example, a one- to three-year-old being sometimes allowed to scream for what he wants and be generally uncontrolled, and sometimes severely punished for the same behaviour would cause an anal fixation. While at a purely biological level the anal stage of development is associated with toilet training, more broadly it is about the child learning compliant self-control in general. Erratic control of the child by the parent at this stage of his development leaves him in doubt about what is and is not demanded of him, promoting him to fixate some energy around these issues in a bid to resolve them.)

No wonder we all have fixations!

Regression

The stages of development at which we have left substantial amounts of BOUND energy in our FIXATIONS become, for the rest of our lives, places to retreat to when our defence mechanisms are insufficient for us to cope adequately with the ego's current challenges. Behaviour associated with a (FIXATED) earlier level of development is termed regression, which is in the service of the presently suffering ego.

In the short term, regression may offer the ego relief; but, prolonged, it is likely to defeat its own purpose, for it then compels the ego to re-experience the anxiety associated with the time when the FIXATION was established.

The commonplace reversion to crawling and babbling like a baby rather than walking and talking, in a two-year-old child, in response to the extreme UNPLEASURE she experiences at the birth of a sibling is an example of regression. In grown-ups, smoking and other addictions, in their components of immediate relief from tension *and* the anxiety they bring in their wake, exemplify well the mixed blessing of regression.

PATHOLOGY

From all that has been said in this chapter so far it is evident that psychological health is a relative matter. Nevertheless, in broad terms, health is a matter of having achieved a satisfactory degree of harmony between id, ego, and superego. Conversely, when the three systems of self are sufficiently at odds with one another that the individual is dissatisfied with herself and the world, and her efficiency is reduced, she is said to be maladjusted.

Neurosis and psychosis

Neurotic illnesses are those in which the symptoms of dis-ease in the individual are incapable of an ORGANIC explanation but which, with the exception of traumatic neuroses (such as a life-threatening accident or being raped), are capable of being interpreted as having unconscious causes. Incapacitating stammering which has no ORGANIC cause is an example of physical debility which warrants searching for its unconscious meaning. All kinds of PHOBIAS (in which acute fear is focused on an object or action that is non-threatening) are also examples of neurotic illness.

The term neurosis is usually confined to illness in which the ego remains intact, in contrast to psychosis, in which the defence mechanisms have been insufficient to maintain the ego's integrity, and the person is no longer functioning in accordance with the REALITY PRINCIPLE (such as hearing voices telling him he is the true Messiah).

Anxiety
Anxiety is the principal signal which forewarns the ego of an impending threat to its equilibrium. Anxiety (or fear) can have its basis in reality, for example, if we are in imminent danger from a rush of oncoming traffic while we are crossing the road. But most anxiety is NEUROTIC anxiety, that is, fear which is aroused by a perception of danger from the INSTINCTS. NEUROTIC anxiety is much more of a burden on the ego than objective anxiety which gets resolved by appropriate fight or flight responses to external danger. NEUROTIC anxiety continues unresolved.

Symptoms
In NEUROSIS, anxiety may be accompanied by other symptoms of dis-ease. Symptoms are the expression of inadequate compromise formations between conflicting forces in the psyche. They are not, in themselves, sufficient to define the content of the dis-ease. By analogy with symptoms of physical disease, for example, a man may limp because he has one leg shorter than the other, or because he has 'pins and needles' in his leg, or because he has had a stroke; enquiry is needed to decide the cause.

Consider a forty-two-year-old man who has been an increasingly successful salesman for the past twenty years and now seeks psychotherapy because he has suddenly become unable to 'close his deals'. As he begins to reveal himself in therapy he might disclose, for example, that he is now the same age as his father was when he died and he, the son, cannot bring himself to fulfil his potential for longer than his father was able to. Or that, despite being a successful salesman, he really always wanted to be a lawyer, and is now setting himself up to lose his job so he can do a law degree before he believes it will be too late to start. Or, having been unfaithful to his wife over the past six months, he is punishing himself with symbolic impotence. Or …

Many people seek psychotherapy only when they develop an overwhelmingly incapacitating symptom and tell the therapist they 'only' want to get rid of that symptom. The therapist often has to work hard to persuade the client that this is not possible; the underlying meaning needs to be discovered and articulated, after which the symptom will disappear of its own accord.

Repression

The last resort of the ego in response to its pain in the face of unresolved conflict of impulses between itself and the id or between the id and the superego is repression. In repression, the offending impulse is forced out of consciousness in a bid to be relieved of it.

When it is effective, repression can indeed restore the whole system of the self to equilibrium and a reduction in anxiety; but repression pays the price of tense, guarded rigidity and may produce debilitating somatic (i.e. bodily) symptoms. Withdrawing big chunks of instinctual awareness from the ego leads to a profoundly impoverished life. Thus, paradoxically, manifest anxiety, which is so painful and so disruptive of a person's everyday functioning is generally a sign of lesser pathology than the stultified equilibrium of the person who has repressed large chunks of his instinctual energy. To the psychoanalyst, manifest anxiety is a valuable sign of the vulnerable accessibility of the psyche to reorganisation; whereas the severely repressed person may need to be *made* anxious before any improvement in his health can be vouchsafed. The theory of Transactional Analysis makes vivid how pathology can, paradoxically, become greater and harder to treat as anxiety diminishes.

RECOMMENDED READING

Rycroft, C (1995) *Critical Dictionary of Psychoanalysis*. London: Penguin.
Frankl, VE (2004) *Man's Search for Meaning.* London: Rider.

5

THE DEVELOPMENT OF
PERSONALITY AND CHARACTER

Orthodox psychoanalysis defines the essentially immutable development of personality and CHARACTER as occurring in three well-defined stages between birth and six years of age. These stages are named the oral stage of development (roughly birth to eighteen months), the anal stage (roughly eighteen months to three years), and the genital (Oedipal) stage (roughly three to six years). In these three stages, LIBIDO is essentially focused respectively on the mouth, the anus and the genitals, these organs being regarded primarily as sources of pleasurable sensations.

However, since the 1930s, all schools of psychoanalysis have increasingly regarded these bodily organs not so much as intrinsic sources of LIBIDINOUS satisfaction but rather as the instrumental means by which the child's relationships to its parents and the world of objects are developed.

In this chapter (and in Chapter 6) I will be describing the stages of development in terms of the phenomenal growth of the infant and young child's relationship to its parents and the physical world.

In this book, I will use the word 'personality' when describing those aspects of the self that are attributable to the combination of innate predispositions (that part which is given by nature or CONSTITUTIONAL) and conditioned adaptations (that part which is learned) in the growing ego until the age of about three years. CHARACTER will refer to those aspects of self attributable to the imposition of a moral code in the child between the ages of about three and six years of age, which is principally the stage of superego development.

The development of personality and CHARACTER takes place as a result of two major conditions: the MATURATION of natural growth, and learning to overcome frustrations, avoid pain, resolve conflicts, and reduce anxiety.

The means by which human personality development takes

place is probably hard-wired into the brain, as in other species. But while there is much inferential evidence that three to six years of age is biologically programmed as the optimum time for the imprinting of the uniquely human attribute of a moral code, without the explicit imposition of controls and values on the growing child by parents (or other authority figures) the CHARACTER (superego) will be largely a lacuna (i.e. missing), resulting in what, in adult life, is called the 'psychopathic personality'.

PERSONALITY DEVELOPMENT

Birth to six months (oral-sucking stage)
Newborn babies express with unselfconscious explicitness the core id truth that we are utterly self-seeking and care for nothing and nobody as much as our own survival in the first place, and the immediate gratification of our every desire and impulse in the second. Fortunately for newborn babies, the 'maternal instinct', by and large, ensures that mothers are uniquely willing, at this time, to sublimate virtually all of their own ego (as well as id) desires into providing their infant, as far as is humanly possible, with the immediate gratification of its (id) impulses.

The parent's smile is perhaps the single most reinforcing experience the infant has, apart from the satisfaction of its basic needs for the relief of hunger, thirst and pain. The only distinctions the newborn infant makes is between total satisfaction—in which case he is either feeding or asleep—or of total UNPLEASURE, in which case the universe consists wholly of its screaming desire for food or the elimination of other bodily pain.

For newborn babies, the loving skin-to-skin contact given them by their parents is as vital to their survival as food, and most parents instinctively give their babies this, and most babies grow and thrive. A contented baby held lovingly in its mother's arms is the epitome of bliss, to which state of being we all long to return and come closest to in the ecstasy of sexual orgasm with a partner we passionately desire.

The unconditional, self-denying love that a healthy mother gives her newborn baby effectively says to the baby, 'I love you because you are you, irrespective of anything you do to please or displease me'. This is the basis of the child experiencing trust in the essential benevolence of the universe, which is the necessary precondition for the healthy progress of the child through all the other developmental stages to maturity. Between birth and about six months, babies are undifferentiated id.

Six months to one year (oral-biting stage)
In the second half of the first year of life the child begins to 'know' things and she is pre-eminently motivated to know more through her exploration of the environment. But her 'knowing' is still much more PRIMARY than SECONDARY PROCESSING (for definitions see Chapter 3, pp. 23–4). She knows she can please her mother by eating, for which she is rewarded with smiles, so her mouth continues to be her prime weapon in commanding the world as she knows it.

The exploratory DRIVE from six to twelve months is the foundation of the child's lifelong capacity for joyous play and creativity, and inhibiting him now will permanently inhibit his spontaneity and his creativity later in life. (It has actually been shown that children of about seven or eight years of age who were, as infants, regularly confined in playpens, are less competent at reading and writing than those who were not so imprisoned.)

The child now knows he is a separate being from his mother and he is poignantly aware of his dependence on her for his survival. He now experiences his first real fear—that his mother will abandon him—manifest as 'separation anxiety', which reaches its peak between about eight and ten months of age as the REALITY PRINCIPLE begins to emerge. To make his fear of abandonment tolerable, toward the end of the first year of his life the child learns to enjoy playing 'peek-a-boo', through which he pretends his mother has left him, but he makes her come back, at his bidding, when he takes his hands away from his eyes. The tension of his fear is dissolved in the ensuing laughter. This game continues to be played by human beings throughout their lives in the thrills they get from *pretend* life-threatening experiences, such as riding a roller coaster.

Oral FIXATIONS arise when this stage of development is not satisfactorily achieved (see pp. 31–2) and consequently some libidinous energy remains BOUND at this level of the personality. Oral FIXATIONS are manifest in such TRAITS and habits as greed or abstemiousness; having a 'biting tongue'; being an 'all-mouth' high-pressure salesman or, conversely, being timid, shy, and unforthcoming; being gluttonous; smoking; chewing gum. Any of these TRAITS can be commonly observed in everyday life. They are NEUROTIC (see pp. 33–4) when they become debilitatingly dominant in the personality.

One to three years (anal stage)

The true ego is now beginning its emergence and the child's use of the pronoun 'I' affirms this. (There is all the difference in the world between, 'Baby want dolly' and 'I want my doll'.)

In the interests of the child's safety and SOCIALISATION, and the preservation of the parents' sanity, the as yet untamed ego has to be contained by others before the child has a developed superego to do this for himself, internally. This is achieved by a large number of inhibiting 'Don'ts' imposed both verbally and physically on a child at this stage of development because the child has neither the knowledge nor the care and consideration for himself or others that would enable him voluntarily, for example, not to tear up his parents' books, not to scream for what he wants, not to jump off a sixth-floor balcony. So at this stage parents are bound to inculcate *fear of retribution* into their child, with sufficient power that the child internalises their punitive wrath in his own mind.

An angry look or forceful bodily removal of the child, accompanied by 'Don't touch the stove', 'Don't pull the cat's tail', 'Don't scream', 'Don't pick your nose', 'Don't take ...', 'Don't hurt ...' are quickly internalised by the child, after which he *automatically* responds to these prohibitions even when his parents are not around. If he disobeys a prohibition, he no longer needs Mother or Father to stop him or give him an angry look; he stops himself by giving himself the appropriately inculcated bad feeling previously imposed on him by his parents, and may even remonstrate aloud with himself, such as by shaking his head and saying, 'No, no', by the time he gets within two feet of the stove, the cat's tail, etc.

This simple, mindless obedience is the *precursor of the superego*, but it lacks the moral justifications that are attached to true superego precepts and inhibitions. The one- to three-year-old is, of necessity, constrained by overt punishment and the fear of it. But by the time he is about six years old he will *understand the reasons* for the self-preservative constraints imposed on him, and *understand the justifications* for the 'Do unto others ...' constraints imposed on him earlier. Then his conscience will be his guide, which will be supported by his ego against the unBOUNDED impulses of his instincts.

While good parents do their best, at least sometimes, to give the one- to three-year-old child reasons and justifications for the restraints they impose on her at this stage of her development, she is barely capable, if at all, of understanding these reasons and justifications. So what is mostly being instigated by parents is powerful REPRESSION of unacceptable impulses exhibited by the child, and, to this extent, these impulses are likely to be repressed in the child for the rest of his life. Such REPRESSIONS are good to the extent that they will *permanently* inhibit the child from such self-destructive activities as crossing a road without looking both ways first, putting his hands in fire, etc. They are also good to the extent that, as the precursor of the EGO IDEAL, he learns *always* to say please and thank you and generally have 'good manners' towards others.

But REPRESSIONS are bad for the child's lifelong psychological health to the extent that some of the controls imposed on him are unnecessary to his or others' well-being, but are given by parents in accordance with their own *NEUROTIC inhibitions*. And, being human, all parents are bound to transmit some such unnecessary REPRESSIVE constraints on their child.

The NEUROTIC 'don'ts' that parents inflict on the child at this stage of her development are, as often as not, transmitted covertly and non-verbally (and so more powerfully, because actions speak louder than words). For example, a child pushed away when she tries to clamber onto her father's knee probably receives the

REPRESSIVE message, 'Don't be close', and she is always likely to have difficulty in forming intimate relationships. An embarrassed look on the face of a mother whose child says, 'I hate my brother', is likely to be received as, 'Don't express bad feelings', and the child is likely to be rigidly polite and inauthentic in her emotional expressiveness for the rest of her life. An angry look given to a child who praises himself for something he has done well, is usually taken to mean, 'Don't succeed', and he is likely chronically to judge himself a failure, irrespective of his actual accomplishments. And a disgusted look given to a child who has accidentally soiled his pants most likely means, 'Don't feel good about yourself', and this child will grow up to be a perfectionist who chronically feels guilty about his own behaviour and is critically blemishing of other people as well.

While it is probably the case that only a minority of parents scrupulously and self-consciously seek to avoid passing on their own NEUROTIC inhibitions to their child, all normally loving parents instinctively make an effort more often to protect and socialise their children by rewards rather than punishment. But many don't realise that, for example, 'Mummy is cross with you when you make a lot of noise' will as surely create a grown-up woman who *is* noisy (*and* feels bad about herself for this) as 'What a good girl being so quiet' will create a grown-up woman who is generally quiet (*and* feels good about herself for this). Ideally, of course, the naturally noisy child needs to be made to feel OK about being noisy, which might be helped, for example by being praised for his vociferous cheering at a sporting event.

Between the ages of one and three, alongside the crucially significant REPRESSION of id impulses that are unacceptable to parents, the child's ego is rapidly developing; his reasoning ability is emerging and is expressed in the acquisition of much objective knowledge and skills, in accordance with the REALITY PRINCIPLE. His growing, self-sufficient competency is manifest in many practical skills, such as fully feeding himself, building a tower of blocks, blowing his nose, pouring water from one container into another, and, above all else, in the acquisition of language.

Emotionally, in accordance with the REPRESSIVE restraints

forcefully imposed on his id by his parents, his self-esteem is based on his *obedient control of his impulses*, including, as Freud pointed out, the control of his bladder and sphincter muscles, by which means he generally receives abundant praise from his mother.

Anal FIXATIONS arise when this stage of development is not satisfactorily completed. Anal stage FIXATIONS are manifest as 'OBSESSIVE-COMPULSIVE' behaviour or attitudes, in such personality TRAITS as obstinacy, orderliness, meanness and parsimony and equally by compulsive pliancy, untidiness, generosity and extravagance. Again, any of these TRAITS can be commonly observed in everyday life and they are NEUROTIC when they become debilitatingly dominant in the personality.

CHARACTER DEVELOPMENT

Three to six years (genital stage)

This stage of development is often termed the 'Oedipal' stage after the mythical Oedipus who killed his father and married his mother without knowing that they were his parents. The relevance of this myth to the three- to six-year-old level of development first arose in Freud's mind out of the self-analysis he conducted after the death of his father. The Oedipus complex made its first published appearance in *The Interpretation of Dreams* (1900/ 1967). The term was first applied to boys, the equivalent in girls being the *Electra complex*.

Between the ages of three and six every girl falls in love with her father, wants to get rid of her mother in order to possess him, and has to come to terms with the realities that she can neither possess her father nor get rid of her mother. She is forced to *compromise* her desires and, ideally, she reconciles herself to her frustration by deciding, 'When I grow up I am going to be a lady like Mummy and marry a man like Daddy.'

Between the ages of three and six every boy falls in love with his mother, wants to get rid of his father in order to possess her, and has to come to terms with the realities that he can neither possess his mother nor get rid of his father. He is forced to *compromise* his desires and, ideally, he reconciles himself to his frustration by deciding, 'When I grow up I am going to be a man like Daddy and marry a lady like Mummy.'

Thus the child transforms his or her perception of his or her same-sexed parent as an aggressive rival for the love of his or her opposite-sexed parent by 'IDENTIFYING with the aggressor' and she/he transmutes her/his desire to possess the opposite-sexed parent into the EGO IDEAL she/he will later seek in an *available* other. This process is at the core of the formation of the true superego, containing, as it does, conscience and the EGO IDEAL.

The parents' roles at this stage of the child's development demand that they, too, express the best possible *compromise* between reinforcing the child's sexual self-esteem while denying it the specific gratification it presently seeks. The boy wants to feel that his mother loves him more than she loves his father; the girl want to feel that her father loves her more than he loves her mother. It is imperative that the child be defeated in this aim. The child experiencing him- or herself to be the victor in this battle is one of the greatest tragedies that can occur with respect to his or her subsequent lifelong ability to form satisfying relationships with the opposite sex and, indeed, to establish and maintain a satisfying self-image and satisfactory attitudes to the world of other people and life in general.

The Oedipal battle, played out by Mother, Father and child is overwhelmingly the most deterministic experience in the formation of our CHARACTER and our relationship needs and propensities for the rest of our lives. For essentially healthy functioning throughout his or her life, the Oedipal battle must be lost by the child.

On the other hand, the subsequent healthy self-esteem of the child also depends on the receipt of a loving response from the opposite-sexed parent to his or her crypto-sexual (i.e. coded) overtures. While there are, of course, huge variations amongst individuals, stereotypically, at this stage, a girl wants her father to express admiration for her looks, her clothes and to pay homage to her sweetness and charm; and a boy wants his mother to express admiration for his attempts to impress her with his strength, bravery and power. Thus, when Daddy comes home from work and his daughter rushes to kiss him before Mummy can, a loving mother understandingly allows this to happen, and a loving father plays with his daughter for a while before firmly telling her that it is time for them to stop playing because he wants to talk to and cuddle Mummy. And when Daddy comes home from work, a loving mother insistently pushes her son away from her, telling him that she wants to be with Daddy now that he has come home, but that, after dinner, *Daddy* will play with him, thus counterbalancing her son's attachment to her in favour of his IDENTIFICATION with his father.

From this prototypical scenario it is evident that girls' and boys' experiences of the Oedipal stage are not symmetrical. Both girls and boys need to be granted some gratification of their possessive attachment to their opposite-sexed parent, while at the same time being somewhat coercively propelled into relinquishing that possessiveness in favour of modelling themselves, by IDENTIFICATION, on the attributes of their same-sexed parent. But both boys and girls typically spend much more time with their mothers than their fathers, so a boy's possessive attachment to his mother is likely to be greater than a girl's possessive attachment to her father. In the ordinary course of events, a boy has to struggle harder to free himself from his mother and attain his sexual autonomy than a girl has to struggle to free herself from her father and attain her sexual autonomy. When, for whatever reason, a boy is overwhelmed by his SYMBIOTIC attachment to his mother it *may* account for his becoming homosexual. And the generally easier task for a girl of separating from her father may, to some extent, account for the greater prevalence of male over female homosexuality. (However, there is considerable evidence that innate CONSTITUTIONAL FACTORS play a large part in determining homosexuality, irrespective of any conditioning in favour or contrary to it.)

What emerges out of all of this is the child's CHARACTER, through the emergence of his or her superego, enabling him or her appropriately both to control and nourish his or her own and other's aggressive and sexual impulses in the light of *recognition of the need to compromise between his or her own and others' desires*. The child is now able appropriately sometimes to feel responsible or guilty and sometimes righteously to blame others. The child is also now capable of sharing and caring responses towards other people, and a considerable degree of self-discipline in maintaining his or her own general well-being. Now he understands the justifications for many of the prohibitions that were imposed on him from one to three years old which, at that time, he was made non-comprehendingly simply to obey. Now he fears the retribution of his own superego conscience as much as the withdrawal of the love of his mother and father.

Also at this time, with his or her newly acquired moral code, the child's behaviour is broadened by virtue of *added flexibility* through dialogue the superego may have with the ego. For example, as a two-year-old he may have been made to accept that he was *never* allowed to eat chocolate after his bath time, and he fearfully obeyed this prohibition just because Mummy or Daddy said so. Now, as a six-year-old, he understands the *general principle* that sugar causes tooth decay, which must be protected against by tooth-brushing, so he may quite self-righteously choose to eat some chocolate after bath time—at which time he has brushed his teeth—so long as he brushes his teeth (again) after eating the chocolate. A two-year-old may 'share' some chocolate with her doll and 'eat it for her', but a six-year-old is capable of truly sharing a bar of chocolate with a friend. And a six-year-old is, in principle, capable of understanding such concepts as 'a white lie', where a smaller 'good' is sacrificed to a larger one.

The child also now consolidates his (anal-stage) understanding that 'giving' as well as 'taking' is inevitably demanded of him if he is to receive the loving attention from others he so craves. At the purely biological level of toilet training, the parents' demands for the child to 'let go of' and 'give' them her faeces, and their psychological demands for other obedient self-control, have generally been accepted by the child. The satisfactory completion of the anal stage of development, combined with the child's Oedipal experiences mean that from now on, he or she is implicitly aware that tenderness and aggression have to be balanced in the expression of his or her desire for intimacy with others.

From the evidence of children brought up in orphanages or communes or in the absence of one of their parents, it seems that the Oedipus complex is, at least partly, biologically determined and presents itself in the experience of three- to six-year-old children, irrespective of external reality. There is considerable clinical evidence that, in the absence of one parent, the child will, at this stage of her development, fantasise that parent and create and live through the Oedipus complex as if the missing parent were present.

At the conclusion of the Oedipal stage of development, the child has a moral code. He has had a multitude of experiences during this stage of development involving a huge range of emotions and impulses including love, hate, blame, guilt, envy, jealousy, rivalry, ambition, power, and revenge, which constitute his now-achieved *emotional literacy*. His personality and CHARACTER are complete and everything hereafter will be repetition (see REPETITION COMPULSION Chapter 2, p. 19).

Oedipal FIXATIONS are expressed in unresolved SYMBIOSES with one or both of the parents. Unresolved SYMBIOTIC attachment to the opposite-sexed parent will incline the child, throughout his life, to too much tenderness, that is, to an underdeveloped ability to express lusty sexual desire and eroticism. Unresolved SYMBIOTIC attachment to the same-sexed parent will incline the child, throughout his life, to too much aggression in his or her sexual relationships, that is, an underdeveloped ability to love him- or herself and, therefore, others.

RECOMMENDED READING

Bowlby, J (1955) *Child Care and the Growth of Love*. Harmondsworth: Penguin.

Erikson, EH (1995) *Childhood and Society.* London: Vintage.

Freud, A (1966) *The Psychoanalytic Treatment of Children.* New York: Schocken Books.

Freud, S (1900/1967) *The Interpretation of Dreams*. London: George Allen & Unwin (1967 edition).

6

LATENCY, PUBERTY, ADOLESCENCE
AND BEYOND

Notwithstanding that the human personality and CHARACTER are complete by the end of the Oedipal stage of development and all our experiences thereafter are essentially repetition, there remain some clearly defined further MATURATION processes during which each of the oral, anal and genital stages are repeated, as it were, at a higher level. The original life-plan, determined by the child's experiences up until the age of six, gets overlaid with analogous experiences at his later stage of development, which, as we will see, allows for some opportunity on the part of parents and educators to readjust their input in the earlier stages of development, as well as consolidating them.

SIX TO TWELVE YEARS (LATENCY)

This period of development is called 'latency' in psychoanalytic theory because sexuality (LIBIDO) is temporarily suppressed in favour of intellectual development and social learning through IDENTIFICATION with same-sexed peers. It is as if, recoiling bruised from his or her rejection in love (during the Oedipal stage), the child now seeks compensation by controlling the external world through the REALITY PRINCIPLE by the acquisition of knowledge and competence and the ways of being and doing of his or her same-sexed parent. The pain of love is defended against with a 'yuk!' attitude towards the opposite sex, although the suppression of the heterosexual impulse is far from complete, and 'I'll show you mine if you show me yours' is a popular intermission in the aggressive hostility between the sexes that characterises this stage of development.

Much of the child's healthy development is now in the hands of her teachers, who instruct her and reinforce the culturally demanded skills of literacy, numeracy, and sociability. Subsidiarily, parents typically expand their child's knowledge and interests in the world at large by taking her to pop concerts, football matches, skateboard parks, arranging swimming and music lessons, etc.

In general, the child is a much *less emotional* being now than she ever has been or ever will be again, and is therefore less vulnerable than at any other stage of her development to traumatisation by contingent stresses that may beset her or her family. So now is the best time—if needs be—for parents to separate and divorce, because the child is more able now than at other stages of her development to 'take it in her stride'. (Contrary to much popular misunderstanding, a child's emotional vulnerability to her parents' divorce—or other stressful circumstances—does *not* decrease uniformly with age; twelve to sixteen is probably the most vulnerable age of all.)

But turning away from the quest for (painful) sexual love in favour of autonomous control of the external environment exacts *its* fearful price, too. The quest for omnipotence at this stage of the child's development is poignantly linked to his newly acquired, fully realistic understanding of death. He now knows death's irreversibility and the fact that everybody, including himself, must one day die. He explicitly fears his own death and the deaths of his parents (on whom he still feels he depends for his survival).

His fear of death may be a closely guarded secret, observable only in the many OBSESSIVE-COMPULSIVE rituals, superstitions, and magic rites he surrounds himself with in a fearful bid to 'stop bad things happening'. More defiantly, he may revel in war games, horror stories, violent films and 'Bang, bang, you're dead' games (in which the 'dead' are immediately resurrected!), although girls are more inclined to prefer psychological to physical viciousness. (Freud attributed gender stereotypical behaviours and attributes to the anatomical differences between male and female. In general, his penis inclines a male to express his libidinous impulses through *visibly* potent means; whereas her hidden sexual organs incline the female to express her libidinous impulses in more *covert* ways.) However, these attitudes and activities are only partly successful defences against the fear of death, which is the greatest threat to the child's confidence at this time. Cynicism and depression are more often experienced by a child during this stage of development than is commonly realised.

The writer of this book remembers dealing effectively with one of her daughter's compulsions when she was about ten by exploiting the 'magic' involved, with my own 'greater magic'. My daughter had started compulsively touching doorknobs a certain number of times every time she entered or left a room. I noticed that the number of times she bound herself to touch the doorknobs was steadily increasing and beginning seriously to interfere with her everyday life, as, for instance, in so delaying her that she would miss her bus to school. So I decided that some intervention was called for, and one night as she was going to bed I said, casually (so as not to shame her), 'You know how you keep touching doorknobs?' 'Yes.' 'Do you do it to stop something horrible happening?' Tentatively, 'Yes.' 'Well,' I said, 'I'll tell you why you have to do it. It's because a wicked witch cast a spell on you; but I can undo it because mothers' spells are more powerful than witches'. When I say "Abracadabra" three times you'll never have to touch doorknobs again, and nothing bad will happen to you.' It worked—like a charm!—bearing witness to the child's willingness to revert to PRIMARY PROCESS thinking to be healed even though the REALITY PRINCIPLE of her ego knew full well that witches and spells were 'nonsense'. This form of magical healing is psychologically analogous to belief in God, which grown-ups as well as children may turn to in the face of death and severe pains experienced in life. Freud, however, insistently defined all religious belief as a NEUROTIC illusion—see recommended reading for Chapter 1.

However unspoken a child's fear of death is, parents need to be sensitive to it. If a child does express explicit fear of his own or others' deaths, in normal circumstances a healthy response by parents is something along the lines of, 'Yes, everybody dies one day, but not until they are ready. Mummy and Daddy and you probably won't die for a very, very, very long time, until we've done all the things we want to do.'

Describing death as 'like going to sleep' or 'stopping breathing' may prompt a child to fear going to sleep and/or to fear that unless he self-consciously breathes he will die. The most placatory response to the child's fear of death is probably some form of tautology like, 'You just stop being alive.'

When the death of a loved relative or friend is tragically untimely, there is an added dimension of anger and (irrational) guilt that needs to be expressed by the bereaved survivors, including the child. The death of either parent before the child has reached full maturity—which is actually as late as about thirty years of age—is probably the greatest tragedy that can befall a child. At the deepest level of the child's being, the untimely death of a parent is experienced as overwhelming abandonment which cannot but have profound and permanent psychological consequences for the child. One consequence of the premature death of a parent—especially a child's same-sexed parent—is the child's appreciation of the 'unfairness' of the fact that his parent was not granted enough life to fulfil his or her potential. This perception may seriously inhibit the child in fulfilling his own potential throughout his life; that is, it is as if the child is unwilling to exploit his 'unfair advantage' of more life to live than his parent had and he will probably need psychotherapy to make this inhibition conscious and dissolve it.

TWELVE TO SIXTEEN YEARS (PUBERTY)

At puberty the child is suddenly overwhelmed by a huge surge of sexual-aggressive energy, and manifestly demands its fulfilment as if in infancy again. But he is not an infant and cannot wholly deny the established realities of his ego and superego—his conditioning, reasoning and morality. Much as he might wish, he cannot escape into the naïvety of infancy, but nor are his ego and his superego powerful enough at this stage to contain the insistent demands of his id instincts, which break forth *in defiance of all the REPRESSION that occurred in his one- to-three-year-old self*, which will never again, after this stage, be possible.

In response to all the 'Don'ts' to which s/he was, from one to three, essentially obedient, s/he is now essentially rebellious. Discounting as far as s/he possibly can all the good sense of her ego's reasoning and her superego's conscience, s/he justifies the expression of her sexual and aggressive impulses with the *obverse* of all that s/he was taught from age one to three; all the 'Don'ts' now become 'Do's'. S/he behaves rudely, inconsiderately, and often with scant regard for her own safety and well-being. S/he is much less trustworthy, less reliable, and less sensible than s/he was when s/he was ten. S/he treats her parents with the disdain, contempt and anger due to them as the gaolers s/he perceives them to be. (From the point of view of primitive cultures in which puberty marks the beginning of full maturity and a licence to full sexual expression, we are, indeed, gaolers of our children in our demands that first they have to be educated to achieve the self-sufficiency and autonomy they need in order to function—in our sophisticated culture—independently of parental control.)

The child and her parents are back to the fight between them for *control* that was the core issue of the three- to-six-year-old stage. Then, notwithstanding some obstinacy and temper tantrums on the part of the child, the parents were the clear victors; now, their containment of the pubescent child is tenuous. Their task is to walk the tightrope of tolerating just so much and no more. But since the child now utterly disregards their disapproval, parents have to struggle to find sanctions they can effectively impose on him. Often the granting and withholding of money—which the child now explicitly wants and needs for libidinous display purposes—is the only power parents maintain over the child at this time, and they may use it to manipulate him into minimal acquiescence to their demands of him. Appeals to the child's 'better nature' (superego morality and EGO IDEAL) are a waste of time; his superego has been virtually decommissioned.

Between one and three, before the Oedipal stage of development, obedience was, for the child, generally a small price to pay for the maintenance of the love of his parents, who overwhelmingly provided him with his greatest interpersonal gratifications. Now, post-Oedipally *and* with his newly acquired and overwhelmingly powerful genital sexual impulses, his parents no longer fulfil his most imperative needs. Thus, at this time, it is as if the child regrets having 'given' (in his obedience) to the wrong people, and he seeks to correct this 'mistake' by rebellion against them. Not until he has proudly and happily established a secure sexual relationship for himself will his parents cease to be the threat to his autonomy and sexual gratification that he now perceives them to be. Then, ideally, his relationship with them will revert to the pre-Oedipal quality of asexual mutual love they all once knew. For the time being, the child must struggle through his confusion while his parents poignantly accept the present necessity for things to be as they are. The child should be allowed to feel and express hostility and rebellion, which he now *needs* to do for his healthy development; while, at the same time, the child needs to perceive his parents as *emotionally invulnerable* to his assaults on them and *more powerful* than he is in determining the limits of his rudeness, rebellion, etc. He depends on them to prevent the complete disintegration of his ego and superego. There is only one thing harder than being a pubescent teenager, and that is being the parent of one!

Transitionally, at this stage, in our complexly sophisticated culture, before the child is mature enough *emotionally* to be encouraged to express his full genital sexuality, he finds a temporary salve to his self-esteem through exaggerated IDENTIFICATION with his same-sexed peer group and 'tribal' subdivisions of that peer group. This is comparatively easy for him because it is a natural extension of the same-sexed friendships he became competent in during latency, although this may now precipitate some homosexual impulses, which may be expressed physically but often only emotionally, especially in girls (see p. 48).

The positive corollary to all this very stressful turmoil for child and parents alike is that, with REPRESSION naturally lifted, parents and others have the opportunity to communicate more deeply—albeit turbulently—with the child than will ever again be possible. With effort, parents are given a chance to modify earlier conditioning of their child, if they so desire, before the lid is again firmly shut on the id. There is no more fruitful time for psychoanalysis than now.

SIXTEEN YEARS AND UP (ADOLESCENCE)

Adolescence is the period roughly spanning ages sixteen to twenty-one, when parents are called on to fulfil their final essential role in the rearing of their children to independent adulthood. At this stage, parents are beginning to breathe a sigh of relief that their turbulent, sulky, rude, rebellious, utterly selfish, amoral, dare-devil, couldn't-care-less twelve- to sixteen-year-old is apparently going to be human after all.

Now, all being well, the REALITY PRINCIPLE has been reinstated in the child through some achieved academic credentials and the child is beginning to express some educational or other interests of which the parents basically approve. But the child is still very much at odds with his or her parents. The superego is still unpolished.

The Oedipal battle of the three- to six-year-old stage (of angry rivalry with the same-sexed parent for the love of the opposite-sexed parent) is now being replayed in order to consolidate the superego and, with it, the moral development of the child.

At that earlier Oedipal stage the child was bound, healthily, to lose the battle for supremacy over the same-sexed parent and to feel rejected by the opposite-sexed parent. Now s/he needs to express his or her symbolic revenge on them both by him- or herself rejecting the love of the opposite-sexed parent and angrily competing with the same-sexed parent for power and attractiveness. Thus, when both sides of the coin have been expressed, the child achieves moral maturity by becoming genuinely and fully capable of assessing him- or herself and other people as sometimes 'good' and sometimes 'bad', sometimes culpable and sometimes innocent, sometimes right and sometimes wrong.

Wise and loving parents, secure in their own sexual and other self-esteem, collude with their child's healthy aim to separate himself from his sexual-emotional bonding to them at this stage. Incestuous impulses are felt and must be fought against by both parents and child. An opposite-sexed parent needs insistently *not* to talk about sexual matters to the child and to appreciate and welcome (rather than 'feel hurt' by) the child's expression of revulsion towards intimate contact between them. A same-sexed parent needs constantly to express admiration for the child's accomplishments and attractiveness, and to play down his or her own accomplishments and attractiveness.

However, in general moral matters, the child still needs her parents' loving control for the attainment of a well-enough-developed set of functioning moral standards. She needs to go out into the world equipped with a set of beliefs and values that will stand her in good stead until such time, as an adult established in the larger world, she may safely and assuredly *modify* those parental values in the light of changing realities in her own life.

At this stage the child knows that he still needs his parents to help him achieve this final stage in his functional MATURATION. But because of his struggle against incestuous desire for his opposite-sexed parent and his rivalry with his same-sexed parent— which prompt him to keep a safe distance from both of them—he is resentful of his continuing need of them, and so has to camouflage his need. With his now well-developed capacity for logical reasoning, he initiates arguments with his parents, launching a two-pronged attack on their reasoning and their values, with consummate debating skill and sophistry. But *covertly* he is begging them confidently to *lay down the law* from their own confident value system, so that he may firmly internalise their values and achieve confidence in himself. The last thing he really wants is for them to crumple under his attacks, although manifestly this seems to be the case.

At first, most parents are inclined to fall into the adolescent's trap by responding to his logical attacks on their beliefs and principles with their own logical reasoning; and the child often 'wins' the argument. But, in due course, appropriately wise and loving parents realise what is going on and accept this final essential responsibility of child-rearing, which is insistently to assert the validity of their own beliefs and to discount the relevance of any 'facts' or logic to the contrary. Internally, the child is profoundly grateful, but is unlikely to show it, and will certainly not express thanks to his parents for it until he is confidently established in adult life and has probably become a good and loving parent himself. Then the mutual, safe, asexual love between parents and child, last experienced in the first three years of the child's life, is finally restored.

DEVELOPMENTAL STAGES OF ADULT LIFE

Now the personality and CHARACTER are truly complete and, from now on, the REPETITION COMPULSION rules our lives. We have no choice but to live out what we have become, with the small but significant choice to make the most and the best or the worst and the least of what we are. As Carl Jung put it, 'Free will is doing what I must, gladly.' There is, of course, continuing MATURATION in adult life, even though with much more determined outside of our free will than we are usually willing to admit.

A singular contribution to the psychoanalytic understanding of developmental stages in adult life was made by Erik Erikson (1902–1994). He defined three broad stages of genital (adult) life and delineated them as quests: for intimacy rather than isolation in the young adult; for generativity (i.e. productivity) rather than stagnation in the middle years; and for integrity rather than despair in old age.

RECOMMENDED READING

Bromley, DB (1966) *The Psychology of Human Ageing*. Harmondsworth: Penguin.

Erikson, EH (1950) *Childhood and Society*. Harmondsworth: Penguin.

Hall, CS & Vernon, NJ (1973) *A Primer of Jungian Psychology*. New York: Mentor.

Klein, Mavis (1998) *Understanding Your Child*. London: Piatcus.

Sheehy, G (1977) *Passages*. New York: Bantam.

7

THEORIES AND THERAPIES

Theory as vested interest

A psychological theory tends to define its adherents as vehement enemies of the adherents of any other psychological theory. Certainly there are factions within other disciplines, but less often than in psychology do theoretical differences exert a powerful enough divisive influence to compete with the usual sympathy between people of like interests. All too often psychoanalysts and behaviourists, humanists and experimentalists despise each other, and even Freudians and Jungians and Adlerians or Eysenckians and Skinnerians keep a coldly respectful distance from each other. Thus it is clear that psychologists—of whatever school—often have very strong investments in their chosen profession, and tend to defend against any threat to their relevant points of view.

Theory as language

More positively, different theories may be thought of as different but concordant languages. Within very broad limits, any language is capable of expressing any thought that any human being may wish to utter. From China to the Azores we are all one species. However, environmental conditions, both physical and psychological, have created differences in the *relative* importance and pertinence of various elements in different peoples' experiences of life. And these differences are reflected in the vocabulary of any given culture-language. A centrally important issue will have invoked the creation of minutely discriminating words to match *the need to perceive differences*. Thus the Inuit people, we are told, have about twenty words for our one word 'snow', and Yiddish enables this writer to describe varieties of fools with subtlety and gusto. This seems to be the most valid spirit in which to view various psychological theories. Though we will each, inevitably, be most fluent in our native tongue, a degree of multilingualism in the form of appropriate interpolations of 'foreign' words and phrases can do nothing but enrich our experience and our expressiveness.

HUMANISTIC PSYCHOLOGICAL THEORIES

All HUMANISTIC psychological theories are either directly founded on psychoanalysis or at least bear homage to it in acknowledging the power of the unconscious mind and the profound influence of childhood experiences on adult life. Many HUMANISTIC theories are essentially elaborations of Freud's original concept of the ego.

All useful psychological theories comprehensively account for the ways in which human beings are all alike and the ways in which they differ. Each theory describes our wholeness and dissects that wholeness in its own way, thus revealing a particular cross-section. When we are describing a particular fact about any individual, its best fit is sometimes most vividly displayed in the context of one theory rather than another.

Conversely, insofar as we are all HOLOGRAMS—any part of us can be seen to be representative of our wholeness—given enough attention, we may creatively and inductively develop our own theories. Palmistry, iridology, graphology, physiognomy, reflexology, homoeopathy, acupuncture, blood grouping, astrological sun-signs, phrenology, racial stereotypes, biochemistry, anatomical types, kinaesthesiology, enneagram types ... all bear witness—some more successfully than others—to our intuitive appreciation of our holographic nature. All that is required is a prolonged, fascinated, obsessive concentration on some signs to evolve a coherent theory. A four-foot-six-inch-tall man—who as an actor, was interviewed on television—avowed that he had constructed a reliable personality TYPOLOGY out of his daily observations—from the standpoint of his height—of the shapes of people's nostrils!

FREUD, ADLER AND JUNG

Psychoanalytic theory was developed in the early years of the twentieth century jointly by the most famous three first generation psychoanalysts: Sigmund Freud himself, Alfred Adler, and Carl Jung. For about a decade, all three worked cooperatively and with great intellectual excitement in the elaboration of psychoanalytic theory. Adler joined Freud in 1902 and split from him, more or less amiably, in 1911; but the well-documented and more emotionally intimate relationship which Freud and Jung formed in 1906 ended in tears in 1913. Both Adler and Jung, in their different ways, came to disavow the centrality of the SEXUAL INSTINCT in human MOTIVATION, and founded their own schools, emphasising different core motives.

Alfred Adler (1870–1939)

When Alfred Adler left Freud in 1911 it was to form his own Society of Individual Psychology. Adler believed that the quest for *power* is the primary human MOTIVATION. He developed the theory of *compensation* as an alternative mechanism to Freud's concept of REPRESSION, arguing that individuals develop their lifestyles in a bid to overcome feelings of inferiority. Striving for success, self-assertion and self-aggrandisement reflect both the will to power and its obverse, a sense of inferiority. It is to Adler that we owe the term 'inferiority complex'.

Compensation can be favourable or unfavourable. For example, a childhood lisp might—favourably—be overcome and be associated in adult life with being a talented public speaker; or—unfavourably, with *over-compensation*—a demagogic tyrant.

Adler's overall approach was more rationalistic and optimistic than Freud's. He placed most emphasis on the self-preservative rather than the SEXUAL INSTINCT. Mental disorders of every sort were conceived of as being caused by the construction individuals give to the meaning of their situations. Aggression was particularly emphasised, and symptoms were seen as attempts to safeguard self-esteem and current lifestyle.

He believed birth order had a profound influence on

personality and CHARACTER development, including the observation that 'first children remain forever power-hungry conservatives'.

Adler's Society of Individual Psychology was particularly expansive between 1920 and 1935 and although his fame in recent decades has been overshadowed by the increasing popularity of Jungian ideas, he has had a marked and continuing influence on existential theories of personality and pathology, and his ideas are also common currency in contemporary COGNITIVE and problem-solving theories. In particular the excessive competitiveness that many people experience in everyday contemporary life can be especially well illuminated and addressed by Adlerian theory and therapy.

Carl Jung (1875–1961)

Like Adler, Jung objected to Freud's insistent placement of sexuality at the centre of human MOTIVATION. For Jung it is the quest for *meaning* that is the core goal of life, and he formulated this quest in terms that eventually came quite close to mysticism, despite his perception of himself as an empirical scientist. He insisted that life is a meaningful adventure, whereas Freud insisted that we are simply propelled by our biology, through life, which ends in death and nothingness.

To Freud's conscious, pre-conscious and unconscious components of the mind Jung added the concept of the COLLECTIVE UNCONSCIOUS. He thus divided the unconscious mind into *personal* and *collective* components. The COLLECTIVE UNCONSCIOUS is a phylogenetic (evolutionary) heritage in which traces of ancestral experience lived through down the ages are innately imprinted on the mind as symbolic images (or *ARCHETYPES*).

Jung argued that the explicit quest for meaning for an individual was appropriate to the second half of life, after the ego has been developed and the individual becomes ready to spiritualise his life. He associates this transition with the 'mid-life crisis' that he observed in many of his patients who were otherwise well-integrated and successfully functioning in the wider world.

Jung developed a very impressive personality TYPOLOGY through his elaborated understanding of 'extraversion' (that is, the tendency to be primarily responsive to external stimuli and other people) and 'introversion' (that is, the tendency to be primarily responsive to subjective stimuli in one's own mind)— terms which had been in use since the nineteenth century— combined with the functions *of thinking, feeling, sensing and intuiting*.

He also developed the concepts of *anima* (the unconscious feminine component in the male psyche) and *animus* (the unconscious male component in the female psyche), arguing that, by middle age, these unconscious ARCHETYPES should have become part of the consciousness of men and women in their quest for 'wholeness'.

Jung called his overall theory 'Analytical Psychology', which has become increasingly popular in recent decades in association with many 'new age' trends in the contemporary ZEITGEIST.

MAJOR POST-FREUDIAN PSYCHODYNAMIC THEORISTS

Melanie Klein (1882–1960)

Melanie Klein (no relation of this author) was a pioneer of *child analysis*. She remained within the fold of orthodox Freudian *psychoanalysis* but differed in some fundamental respects from classical theory. She had a special interest in depression and its connection with the oral stage of development. She was much influenced by Karl Abraham's 'OBJECT RELATIONS' theory (see below).

Mother and feeding infant were at the centre of her conceptual picture, and later relationships came to be interpreted in terms of that one. She held that the crucial DRIVE in infancy is the innate aggressive tendency of the baby, which leads him into intolerable conflict over love and hate, from which he tries to escape by PROJECTING the aggressive part of himself onto the outer world— initially the 'good breast' and the 'bad breast' of the mother. Healthy maturity consists of the reconciliation of these in a perception that all human beings are a tolerable mixture of good and bad.

She emphasised the DEATH INSTINCT (see Chapter 2, p. 18 for

definition and description) and proposed that the superego is present long before the Oedipal stage of development. She avowed that the human psyche is in constant oscillation between Eros (LIBIDO) and THANATOS (the DEATH INSTINCT). She called the state of the psyche when Eros is dominant the 'depressive position'; and the state of the psyche when THANATOS is dominant the 'schizoid position'. (Broadly speaking, the depressive position represents a dominance of the superego in the psyche, the schizoid position a dominance of the id.)

Karl Abraham (1877–1925)

Karl Abraham is most famous for introducing the term 'OBJECT RELATIONS' into the vocabulary of psychoanalysis, and the concept continues to be much used in contemporary psychodynamic theory and therapy. The term 'object' had been used early on by Freud to denote the person (or thing) required in order to mediate instinctual discharge, but Abraham elaborated this by connecting difficulties with 'objects' at different stages of development with particular types of subsequent pathology.

So, for example, undischarged LIBIDO at the oral stage of development is likely to be directed against the self, resulting in a depressive-type personality; whereas undischarged LIBIDO at the Oedipal stage of development is more likely to be PROJECTED against an external 'object', say, for example, mice, resulting in a later PHOBIC-type personality.

Anna Freud (1895–1982)

Anna Freud was the youngest of Freud's six children and the only one to follow in her father's footsteps. She escaped Nazi persecution and came from Vienna to London, with her parents, in 1938. In 1945 she established the Hampstead Child Therapy Clinic, where she worked until her death. She is best remembered for her development of the defence mechanisms, which played a big part in the development of 'EGO PSYCHOLOGY' in all its branches.

Karen Horney (1885–1952)

Karen Horney differed from many psychoanalytic writers of her time in the belief that too much emphasis was placed on childhood, to the neglect of the influence of cultural conditions in forming NEUROTIC patterns in people's lives. She delineated three broad categories of coping mechanisms that people variously use in getting their needs met within the context of culture and society. These coping mechanisms are *compliance*, *aggression* and *withdrawal*.

Ronald Fairbairn (1889–1964)
Ronald Fairbairn re-worked and elaborated Abraham's concept of 'OBJECT RELATIONS' into a comprehensive theory. In particular, he held that REPRESSION led to crippling 'SPLITTING' of the ego, especially through keeping at bay highly sexualised and highly dominant figures in the psyche, with which the individual has been unable to cope. For example, inability to cope with hostile feelings towards a parent may result in, 'I love my parent (but) I fear dogs and am angry with my neighbour.'

Donald Winnicott (1896–1971)
Like Fairburn, Winnicott emphasised 'EGO SPLITTING' as a consequence of the child's inability to cope with parents' demands. He coined the much used term 'transitional object' (a teddy bear or other toy or object) which the child clings to in the process of separating from mother. He was a paediatrician and is also well-known for coining the phrase 'good enough mother'.

Erich Fromm (1900–1980)
Erich Fromm was a practising psychoanalyst who developed psychoanalysis in a social context and popularised it in the books he wrote for a lay readership. He emphasised human beings' 'higher' existential needs (as had Jung), particularly through the quests for *love* and *freedom*, which are resisted by the majority of mankind through fear of the responsibilities they entail.

John Bowlby (1907–1990)
John Bowlby emphasised even more than Winnicott the supreme importance of an adequate early mother–child relationship. He

developed 'attachment theory', which deals with the complex mechanisms by which human beings, like other social animals, become attached to each other, and the consequences when these ties are severed. His influence continues to be very great in child psychotherapy and in social work training.

Abraham Maslow (1908–1970)

Abraham Maslow was also a practising psychoanalyst who famously delineated his theory of a hierarchy of needs from physiological, to safety, belonging, esteem, SELF-ACTUALISATION and, finally, Being.

Eric Berne (1910–1970)

Eric Berne was an orthodox psychoanalyst who became impatient with the slowness of psychoanalysis as therapy, and decided that people could be effectively understood and their dis-eases healed *quickly* by reference to the easily accessible conscious ego, rather than probing for deeply repressed material, which takes years on the psychoanalytic couch to reveal. Out of his concentration on the ego he became aware of three primary structures in the ego which he called the 'Parent', 'Adult' and 'Child' ego states, for which discovery he paid homage to the work of Fairbairn. Out of this core concept, Transactional Analysis was developed by Berne and his many followers into a fully comprehensive theory of child development, personality, pathology and psychotherapy, which has also been highly successful in educational and business settings. Transactional Analysis is the subject matter of Chapter 8.

PSYCHODYNAMIC THERAPIES IN GENERAL

What is therapy?

Psychodynamic therapy's aim is to help people find out what they want and then help them to get it. The former task is almost always by far the most prolonged. Finding out what people want involves discovering the idiosyncratic *meanings* of their symptoms—symptoms which may be both physical and psychological. The pursuit of meanings involves microscopic analysis, that is what in everyday life would be called 'making mountains out of molehills'. Thus therapy consists in large measure of the continuing refinement of diagnosis. Revelation is the goal.

Orthodox psychoanalysis stops when revelation is considered complete. All HUMANISTIC therapies recognise the centrality of meaning to a client's dis-ease, but most contemporary, ego-oriented psychodynamic therapies also coach clients in the behavioural changes they need to make to fulfil their wants, pursuing meaning and adaptive behavioural change hand in hand.

MAJOR SCHOOLS OF PSYCHODYNAMIC THERAPY

All psychodynamic therapies assume that the conditioning of the individual in infancy and early childhood is an important determiner of the individual's lifelong propensities to respond to life in the ways she does. And all therapies assume the necessity for—one way or another—undoing faulty conditioning. All therapies also propound—at least implicitly—principles of conservation and flow of energy. Somewhere in every psychodynamic therapy is the notion of energy flowing freely in health and being blocked in pathology. By analogy with his near contemporary, Albert Einstein, Freud sees human beings as, ultimately, like the rest of the universe: interchangeable matter and energy.

Orthodox Freudian Psychoanalysis, Jungian Analytical Psychology, Adlerian Individual Psychology and Kleinian Analysis are all available from the institutes that bear their names (see Appendix, pp. 113–14).

Amongst the large variety of 'post-Freudian' ego-oriented psychotherapies available, differences are essentially differences of focus, and many practitioners consider themselves to be eclectic.

Classical psychoanalysis

In a classical psychoanalytic therapy the analyst remains psychologically remote and essentially silent, offering only occasional interpretations. The aim is to establish the *TRANSFERENCE relationship*; the client eventually resolves her deep-seated conflicts over a period of months or years of analysis, often taking place several times a week.

Classical psychoanalysis can be used in both individual and group therapy. In group therapy, some analysts focus on each of the individuals within the group; other analysts focus on the analysis of the group as a whole family of children in relation to the 'parent' analyst.

Jungian analysis

Jungian analysis is favourable to those clients who are essentially coping well with life but feel the distress of an apparent lack of *meaning* in their lives. The analyst and client are considered partners in the process of finding the idiosyncratic meanings of life for the client through bringing to the surface the *metaphors and symbols* in the client's mind, as yet unrealised by him.

Jungian analysis makes much use of *dream analysis* and other actively *imaginative processes*, such as drawing and painting and the symbolic analysis of *fairy tales and myths*. For some clients, a religious dimension in their lives is also activated.

Adlerian therapy

Adlerian therapy offers a vigorously optimistic approach to the client, making use of *rational dialogue* to unfold insights and find new solutions to problems. The analyst and client develop a friendly relationship between equals, together disentangling contradictions in the client's mind, and turning vagueness into clarity and concreteness.

Adlerian analysis avoids, as far as possible, the dependency of the TRANSFERENCE relationship. Instead, boosting the client's self-esteem, especially through challenging her feelings of *inferiority* and discouragement deriving from the overly perfectionistic ideals she measures herself against. The client is addressed in the context of her whole life, including her intimate and social relationships, rather than focusing on her internal conflicts.

Gestalt therapy

Gestalt therapy focuses on *perceiving, feeling and acting*. It avoids conceptualising and intellectual interpretations. Its main method is dialogue, in which clients often engage in *two-chair work*—that is, talking to imagined significant others or different feelings in himself in an empty chair facing them, and then moving to that chair and responding. For example, if the client's presenting symptom is his headaches, and the therapist perceives that he is also very resentful towards something or somebody, the therapist might ask the client to sit in one chair as if he *is* his headache and talk to his resentment, imagined in the other chair. Then the client is asked to move to the other chair and, this time as his resentment, talk back to his headache. The aim of the exercise is to resolve his problem by reconnecting his headaches and his resentment into a new wholeness ('gestalt').

The process insistently concentrates on *what is happening now*, rather than on any content that is being discussed. It emphasises understanding another's point of view without judging, thus achieving new awareness and insight into unresolved psychological conflicts from the past, resulting in a new sense of *wholeness*, replacing a previously divided self.

Bioenergetics

Bioenergetics emphasises the unity of mind and body and understands psychological *defences* to be visible in the *armoury* of chronic *muscular patterns and ways of breathing* that inhibit self-expression. These are examined and modified, feeding back on the associated psychological dis-ease.

Bioenergetics includes a concept of personality types and their associated chronic patterns of physical expression.

Psychodrama

Psychodrama is typically a form of group therapy. *Action methods* are used to enable *past, present and future* events to be explored, making use of a director, an action area and group members. The director supports groups in exploring new solutions to old problems through role play and drama.

Psychodrama aims to create an internal restructuring of dysfunctional mindsets with other people, leading to greater spontaneity and independence.

TABLE OF MAJOR SCHOOLS OF PSYCHODYNAMIC THERAPY

Therapy and Founder	Idiosycratic Terminology	Mode of Therapy	Curative Focus
Psychoanalysis (Freud)	concepts in analyst's head	TRANSFERENCE of unconscious conflicts	new adaptations to reality through clarification and understanding
Analytical Psychology (Jung)	feeling, thinking, intuiting, sensing, shadow, animus, anima	balancing these functions and transcending them	'individuation' and transcendental meaning
Individual Psychology (Adler)	lifestyle, inferiority complex, compensation	positive encouragement, stresses sibling relationships and creative problem solving	self-mastery of the environment
Gestalt Therapy (Fritz Perls)	here, now, feel, want, do, topdog, underdog	emotional acting out; disallows rational interpretations	changing 'can't' into 'won't' into 'will' through feelings
Transactional Analysis (Eric Berne)	Parent, Adult, Child, strokes, script, decisions	therapist and client share rational understanding	disavowing painful conditioning and making new decisions
Bioenergetics (Wilhelm Reich /Alexander Lowen)	grounding	bodywork emphasising musculature and breathing	release of energy into spontaneity and self-expression
Psychodrama (Jacob Moreno)	(no particular vocabulary)	exploration of internal conflict through role play in dramatic action	release of spontaneity and increased rapport in interpersonal relationships

Transactional Analysis

Transactional Analysis is unique in the vividness with which it deploys the vocabulary and grammar of Freudian theory in its therapy. It shares with Adlerian therapy an optimistic, problem-solving orientation and an avoidance of the TRANSFERENCE relationship in favour of encouraging the client to *spontaneity, authenticity* and *autonomy*. It so effectively epitomises the potency of the psychoanalytic model in everyday life that it deserves the next chapter to itself.

On page 67 is a summary table of some of the major psycho-dynamic therapies, in terms of the names of their founders, their idiosyncratic terminologies, modes of therapy, and curative focuses.

RECOMMENDED READING

Abraham, K (1988) *Selected Papers on Psychoanalysis.* London: Karnac Books.

Bowlby, J (1955) *Child Care and the Growth of Love.* Harmondsworth: Penguin.

Bowlby, J (1998) *Attachment and Loss.* London: Pimlico.

Fairbairn, WRD (1952) *Psychological Studies of Personality.* London: Routledge and Kegan Paul.

Freud, A (1968) *The Ego and the Mechanisms of Defence.* London: The Hogarth Press.

Fromm, E (1995) *The Art of Loving.* London: Penguin.

Fromm, E (2001) *The Fear of Freedom.* London: Routledge.

Hall, CS & Nordby, VJ (1973) *A Primer of Jungian Psychology.* New York: Mentor.

Horney, K (1937) *The Neurotic Personality of Our Time.* London: Kegan Paul.

Klein, Melanie & Riviere, J (1964) *Love, Hate and Reparation.* London: Norton.

Maslow, A (1993) *The Further Reaches of Human Nature.* London: Arkana.

Maslow, A (1999) *Towards a Psychology of Being.* London: Arkana.

McGuire, W (ed) (1991) *The Freud/Jung Letters.* London: Penguin.

Winnicott, DW (1990) *Home is Where We Start From.* London: Penguin.

8

TRANSACTIONAL ANALYSIS—
PSYCHOANALYSIS MADE CONSCIOUS

THE ORIGIN OF TRANSACTIONAL ANALYSIS

Transactional Analysis (or TA as it is familiarly called) is the creation of the Canadian-born psychiatrist Eric Berne (1910–1970).

In 1956, after more than a decade of being in a training analysis, the San Francisco Psychoanalytic Institute rejected his application for certification as a psychoanalyst, deeming him 'not ready'. This failure intensified Berne's long-standing ambition to add something new to psychoanalysis, and he now determined to 'show them' with a completely new approach to psychotherapy.

The essential disagreement between Berne and establishment psychoanalysis concerned practice, not theory. He was, and remained all his life, committed to orthodox psychoanalytic theory, but his frustration with the slowness of psychoanalysis as therapy to effect measurable change in his patients made him baulk at the overly passive role demanded of the analyst. He questioned the assumptions behind the 'rules' of psychoanalysis as therapy, and decided that in one respect they were false. Where psychoanalysis insisted that unconscious conflicts must be resolved before manifest personality changes could effectively and permanently be achieved, Berne claimed that patients could be made better *first*—and quickly—and have their underlying conflicts resolved later (if required). Thus, out of a practical concern to cure people quickly, TA came into being and developed as a theoretical elaboration of psychoanalytic EGO PSYCHOLOGY and a systematised approach to ego therapy.

What distinguishes TA from other theoretical elaborations of the ego is that its concepts are direct derivatives of psychoanalysis as a whole. The Parent, Adult, and Child ego states (see below) of TA are exact derivatives of the superego,

ego, and id but describe the here-and-nowness of our conscious lives; what Berne proposed was essentially Freud without the unconscious (see Figure 4, p. 75).

Berne realised that the core existential reality of any human being is accessible through the conscious and pre-conscious ego and can be revealed by a skilled psychotherapist in a few hours rather than a few years!

This is so, argued Berne, because the experiences we have in the later stages of our development are, through the influence of the REPETITION COMPULSION (see pp. 19 & 46), very similar to the primary experiences of the first six years of our lives. And, unlike the repressed experiences of our earliest years (which can take years to tease into consciousness), our most significant experiences after the age of six are available in our pre-conscious minds and can quickly be brought into full consciousness. The established defence mechanisms are the wedges through which the therapist prizes open the mind to make the pre-conscious material fully conscious.

Berne acknowledged that in cases of very severe REPRESSION— that is, where the usual defences of the ego are absent—classical analysis is the only appropriate therapy. In all other cases, conscious dialogue between the ego states is all that is needed to relieve the patient of his psychological ills.

The concept of the ego states and the delineation of their natures is undoubtedly the central genius of TA theory. But what makes TA more than 'psychoanalysis without the unconscious' is its concept of strokes. Strokes are reinforcement, and a singularly powerful component of TA as theory and therapy is the use it makes of its understanding of positive and negative strokes and their equal potency in reinforcing behaviour. That is, contrary to 'common sense', TA knows that punishment does not work. Punishment merely suppresses undesirable behaviour momentarily while it is being inflicted; but in the long run, punishment actually increases the frequency and intensity of the behaviour it seeks to eliminate. Although Berne seemed to be unaware of the fact, his stroke theory is pure operant conditioning (in which behaviour is modified systematically by rewards given and withheld), the learning theory of B.F. Skinner, the proof of which is sufficiently contained in Skinner having used it successfully to teach pigeons to play ping-pong!

Thus TA is a highly successful marriage of the most unlikely bedfellows, psychoanalysis and BEHAVIOURISM.

Eric Berne wrote six books on TA beginning with *Transactional Analysis in Psychotherapy*, first published in 1961, and culminating in *What Do You Say After You Say Hello?*, published posthumously in 1970.

Since January 1971, the official organ of the International Transactional Analysis Association has been the quarterly *Transactional Analysis Journal*, in whose pages TA theory and application have continued to evolve. Many important concepts now familiarly used by TA therapists and teachers were only incipient in *What Do You Say After You Say Hello?*, but fortunately there have been many brilliant followers of Berne in whose minds these ideas have germinated and been brought to life.

THE STRUCTURES AND FUNCTIONS OF PERSONALITY AND CHARACTER

All of us in all of our waking lives are in one or other of three possible ego states. These are not roles, but different real parts of our being. Nor are they synonyms for superego, ego, and id, which are concepts that refer to the unconscious mind. Ego states, by contrast, are phenomenological realities—that is, observable states of being—and are all contained within the conscious or pre-conscious ego. Existentially, we switch from one of these states of being to another throughout our lives, hour by hour, minute by minute, second by second. They are called Parent, Adult and Child and are represented in the diagram overleaf.

Figure 2   The three principal ego states

The Child ego state

The Child ego state contains our feelings. At birth, we have only our Child. When in our Child we cry when we are miserable, laugh when happy. We are all the things a baby is—demanding, self-centred, loving, spontaneous, honest, uninhibited and lovable.

In the course of the first year of our lives the undifferentiated Natural Child relinquishes some of its energy to two other structures called the Little Professor (which is naturally intuitive and insightful) and the Adapted Child (which is learned through inhibitions imposed on the child). By the end of our first year of life our Child ego state consists of three components: the Natural Child, the Little Professor and the Adapted Child. The Natural Child and the Little Professor are biologically programmed and are thus, together, designated the Free Child.

The Little Professor begins its development at about six months of age through the infant's dawning awareness of the separateness of itself from the rest of the universe. It is manifest in the crawling, exploring, and 'getting into things' so typical of the infant from this time on. It is the precursor of the later-developing Adult ego state and so is often referred to as the Adult-in-the-Child and is designated A_1.

The Adapted Child begins its development towards the end of the first year of life when, in the interests of self-preservation and SOCIALISATION, it is necessary for caretakers to impose inhibitions on the Free Child. The contents of the Adapted Child are determined by the particular 'Don'ts' imposed on the child at this stage. The Adapted Child is, by definition, in conflict with the unbridled impulses of the Natural Child and the Little Professor.

It is the precursor of the later-developing Parent ego state and so is designated P_1.

The totality of the Child ego state is designated C_2. At the end of the first year of life the total energy and contents of the psyche are distributed as in the diagram below.

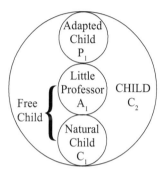

Figure 3   The one-year-old psyche

The Adult ego state
The Adult ego state is our storehouse of facts and skills gained from the objective environment. It is without feeling. It begins its development at about one year of age and has its most rapid development between the ages of about one-and-a-half and three, when it is particularly associated with the child learning to talk; and it has another period of rapid development in latency (about six to twelve years of age). The Adult ego state is designated A_2.

The Parent ego state
The Parent ego state contains our taught concepts of life, the values and generalisations given to us by our parents and other influential people in our lives. When we are in our Parent we are usually behaving like one of our parents did or in accordance with precepts they taught us when young, although our Parent is capable of change and growth throughout our lives. We may reject old values and acquire new ones as a consequence of new experiences and meetings with admired people. Our Parent ego state is essentially

formed in the Oedipal stage of development (three to six years of age) and gets a bit of polishing up in adolescence; but thereafter our Parent is an automatic and therefore a comfortable place to be. The Parent ego state is designated P_2.

The structure of the completed personality and CHARACTER may be summarised in the table below.

Table 1

EGO STATE	CONTENTS
Parent	explicitly taught concepts in general, including values, morality, and generalisations made by the individual herself out of her Child and Adult experiences
Adult	knowledge and skills
Child	innately given feelings and feelings learnt in the process of adaptation to parents' and others' demands

At age six, the ego is structurally complete and can now be placed in the context of the whole self of psychoanalysis, as in Figure 4, below. (In accordance with the psychoanalytic definition of the ego as being largely unconscious, parts of the Parent ego state and of the Natural Child ego state are shown as being in the unconscious realm of the psyche. This figure is a diagrammatic representation of the whole self, not to be interpreted QUANTITATIVELY.)

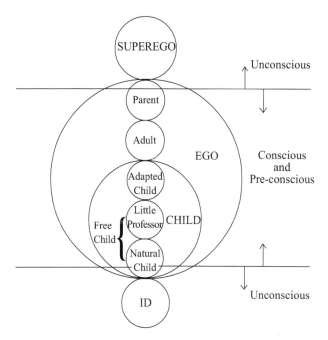

Figure 4   The psychoanalytic and Transactional Analysis
models of the human mind combined

Diagnosis of the ego states

In everyday life most people can readily and quickly acquire the
facility for recognising their own and others' ego states with a
minimum margin of error. The table below delineates some typical
manifestations of the three major ego states, Parent, Adult, and
Child. (In refined analysis, some of the listed characteristics of
the Parent may be discerned as actually being expressions of P_1,
the Adapted Child.)

Table 2 CHARACTERISTICS OF THE EGO STATES

	Parent	Adult	Child
Words	good/bad, should/shouldn't must/mustn't always/ never, right/wrong	how, what, why, when, practical, possible, interesting	wow!, want, can't, won't, wish, hope, please, thank you, I wonder if ..., I have a feeling that ..., That's phoney.
Voice	concerned, comforting, critical	even, calm	free, loud, energetic, whining, excited, pleading
Gestures or Expression	open arms, points finger, frowns, smiles	thoughtful, alert, open	uninhibited, loose, spontaneous, naïve, cute, sad, happy, assertive, whimsical, knowing
Attitude	judgemental, understanding, caring, giving, authoritarian, moralistic	erect, evaluative of facts	curious, compliant, defiant, ashamed, volatile, creative, fun-loving, manipulative, hypothesising

The functions of the ego states

Whereas the structures of the ego states refer to contents specific to the individual, the functions of the ego states refer to various kinds of energy that can be expressed. Broadly speaking, the Parent believes, the Adult thinks, and the Child feels. Summarily, the autonomous functions of the three ego states are as illustrated in Table 3 below.

Table 3

EGO STATE	FUNCTIONS
Parent	believes, protects, controls, directs and nurtures self and others
Adult	thinks, computes, analyses
Child	feels, wants, demands, plays, adapts, fights

The TRILOG

Now apart from the appropriateness of sometimes being in one ego state rather than another, there are also occasions that call for the conscious collaboration of two or more ego states in equal or near-equal measure. Some simple situations are most appropriately experienced in a single, autonomously functioning ego state, for example, writing out cheques (in Adult), riding a roller coaster (in Child), or 'kissing it better' (in Parent). But in many situations in life one ego state is not enough, and the ego states often act collaboratively, in pairs.

The Parent and Adult collaborate to form judgements.

The Parent and Child collaborate to form compromises.

The Adult and Child collaborate to find creative alternatives.

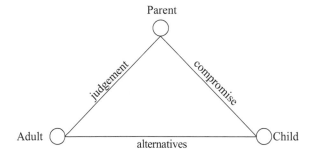

Figure 5 The TRILOG

Examples

Parent–Adult collaboration:

A judge in court combines his knowledge of the actuality of the law (Adult) before making a *judgement* and passing sentence. Should any reader doubt the necessary influence of a judge's Parent, consider the variability of sentences passed for similar crimes by different judges. The awareness of this is expressed in the confidence or trepidation of barristers on behalf of their clients once they know which judge is sitting on their case. 'Harsh' judgements usually imply the judge has a particularly critical Parent, 'lenient' judgements an indulgent Parent, and 'cold' judgements a leaning towards Adult.

Adult–Child collaboration:

A man whose Child yearns for a five-bedroom house on the edge of Hyde Park realizes (Adult) it is beyond his means, so considers and chooses between such alternatives as a five-bedroom house in Wembley or a two-bedroom flat near Hyde Park. A bias towards Adult in setting up alternatives will tend to make the list of options 'cautious', a bias towards Child may make the options 'unrealistic' and their achievement doubtful.

Parent–Child collaboration:

A young woman whose Child would like to exhibit her body as a nightclub stripper compromises with her (disapproving) Parent by becoming an artist's model. Here the collaboration is between two feeling ego states, with no input from Adult, so in terms of actual possibilities, the individual may choose any point on the continuum from all Parent to all Child. But, of course, in terms of the psychological reality, choosing the appropriate degrees of Parent and Child is crucial in determining her sense of well-being. Too much Child in the compromise and the Parent will probably inflict guilt, too much Parent and the Child will be bitter on account of its frustration.

Parent–Adult–Child collaboration:

The most complex and significant of life's decisions—such as marriage, divorce, to have or not to have children—probably all require the harmony of all three ego states for a happy outcome to be achieved. This may account for the emphasis in traditional education—from the ancient Greeks to latter-day British public schools—on the importance of games, since these provide a singular opportunity for training the effective collaboration of all three ego states. Consider a boy playing football. His Parent is obeying the rules, his Adult skills are being exercised, and his Child is having a marvellous time.

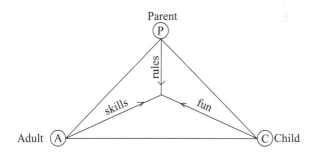

Figure 5a   A boy playing football

TRANSACTIONS AND STROKES

Transactions in general

When two people meet transactions occur between them (even if no words are spoken). The Parent, Adult and Child contained within one skin meet a Parent, Adult and Child contained in another skin. Since either person may choose to be in any of his three ego states and to address any of the three ego states of the other, *there are nine possibilities for any single transaction.*

In everyday life, our reactions to other people are based at least as much on *how* they say what they say as on the literal content of the transaction. This is easy to demonstrate with many simple remarks such as 'What's for supper?' which the reader may practise saying in as many of the nine different ways as possible.

So, with only the stimulus of printed words on a page, it is difficult to define the nature of a transaction unambiguously. Nevertheless, for the record, here are idealised examples of the nine possible types of transaction.

1. Stranger to stranger in the street: 'Excuse me, could you tell me the time?' (Adult to Adult)
2. Boy to girl: 'You're the most beautiful girl I've ever met.' (Child to Child)
3. Husband to wife: 'Shall we take the kids out for a treat this weekend?' (Parent to Parent)
4. Pupil to teacher: 'What should I do next?' (Adult to Parent)
5. Ten-year-old to his parents: 'You stay in bed and I'll make breakfast.' (Parent to Child)
6. Mother to whining three-year-old on the bus: 'We'll soon be home and then you can have some lunch and a nice rest.' (Adult to Child)
7. Father to son: 'You'll never saw a straight piece of wood that way. Here, let me show you how.' (Parent to Adult)
8. Girl to boy: 'You are clever.' (Child to Adult)
9. Woman to man: 'Will you buy me a diamond engagement ring?' (Child to Parent)

Complementary, crossed and ulterior transactions

Now let's consider some pairs of transactions. For example, a husband arrives home from work with a streaming cold. His wife may initiate a transaction with him such as, (a) 'You poor thing. Get into bed and I'll make you a nice hot toddy' (Parent to Child). Or, (b) 'That's a bad cold you've got. There's some aspirin and some vitamin C tablets in the bathroom cabinet if you want them' (Adult to Adult). Or, (c) 'Wow, you've got a corker! Keep away from me. I don't want it', (Child to Child). Or, (d) 'I hope you're not going to go on about this cold. Remember you promised to take me out tonight' (Child to Parent).

What happens next depends on how the husband chooses to respond. If, for example, he responds to (a) with, 'Thank you darling. That's just what I feel like' (Child to Parent) or to (d) with, 'I'm sorry, I'll have to break my promise then' (Parent to

Child), the transactions will have been complementary. The ego state addressed responded to the ego state which addressed it and communication, though not necessarily happy, is clear and straightforward and, as long as it continues *complementarily*, will not result in misunderstandings.

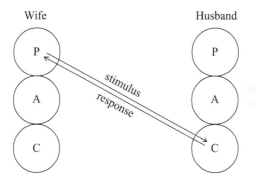

Figure 6 A complementary transaction

Consider, however, the possibility that the husband responds to (b), his wife's stimulus, 'That's a bad cold you've got. There's some aspirin and some vitamin C tablets in the bathroom cabinet if you want them (Adult to Adult) with 'For goodness sake, woman! Don't you realise that once you've got a cold there's nothing you can do about it?' (Parent to Child). The result is a crossed transaction of the commonest kind, where an Adult to Adult stimulus gets a critical Parent to Child response, and communication breaks down. (The vast majority of fights between individuals and nations are precipitated by just such crossed transactions.)

Although the most common crossed transactions are self-evidently defined as such by the actual intersection of the *stimulus* and *response* lines of communication, the category of crossed transactions also includes non-complementary but parallel stimulus and response lines, and some angular relationships between stimulus and response.

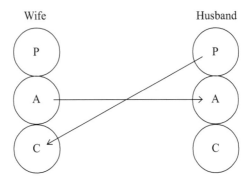

Figure 7   A crossed transaction

For example, if the husband had responded to his wife's Adult to Adult stimulus of 'There's some aspirin and some vitamin C tablets in the bathroom cabinet if you want them' with 'We must get a child-proof lock on that bathroom cabinet' we would have:

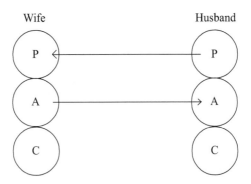

Figure 8   Another type of crossed transaction

Or if he had responded to his wife's 'Get into bed and I'll make you a nice hot toddy' with, 'If you come with me', we would have the situation illustrated in Figure 9.

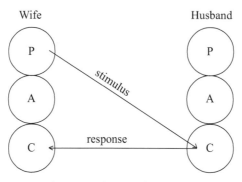

Figure 9   An angular type of crossed transaction

As well as complementary and crossed, there is a third kind of transaction between people, called ulterior. Ulterior transactions are the stuff of which much of our working and social lives are made. They occur when communication nominally takes place between two ego states but, covertly, (i.e. hidden or disguised) at least one other ego state is involved. At the hidden level, at least one Child ego state is usually involved. *The covert stimulus and the covert response always contain the most important part of the communication.* The covert lines of communication are always drawn as dotted lines in transactional diagrams.

Ulterior (covert) transactions are sub-divided into *angular* and *duplex* types. An *angular* ulterior transaction is typically a 'conning' transaction.

Example

Salesman: (Stimulus₁, overt): 'It's a beautiful fit, sir, but perhaps you'd prefer one not so youthful looking.'

(Stimulus₂, covert): 'Buy this if you want to look young.'

Customer: (Response, overt): 'I'll have it.'

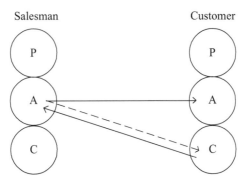

Figure 10   An angular ulterior transaction

Only Stimulus$_1$ is spoken, but the more powerful stimulus is the covert, Adult to Child one in which the salesman aims to 'hook' the Child while himself staying in his cool Adult.

In *duplex* ulterior transactions the Child ego states of both parties are usually involved.

Example

Man: (S$_1$): Would you like to come back to my place for a
                 cup of coffee?
         (S$_2$): Let's have it off at my place.
Woman: (R$_1$): Oh yes. I could do with a cup of coffee.
         (R$_2$): Yeah, let's.

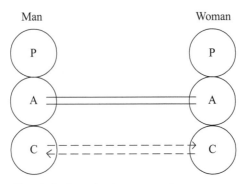

Figure 11   A duplex ulterior transaction

Ulterior transactions may occur for many different reasons, but they all have in common that they provide a face-saving way out to either or both parties. In the example of the man and the woman above, the woman may have replied, 'Thanks, but I'm very tired and I've got an early start in the morning' (Adult to Adult), but meant, 'No, I don't fancy you' (Child to Child), in which case, though her meaning was clear, the situation was resolved with less loss of face for the man and less gracelessness for her than if the Child to Child transaction had been openly expressed. Furthermore, the man was, from the start, protected from the woman repudiating his Child to Child transaction openly. Had she replied overtly 'Buzz off, buster!' (Child to Child), he could hotly deny that he had meant anything more than what was contained in his overt Adult to Adult transaction. Similarly, if the customer in the previous example had replied to the salesman with, 'I'll thank you to mind your manners!' (Parent to Child), the salesman could 'legitimately' reply, 'I beg your pardon, sir. Did I say something wrong?' (Child to Parent).

Thus many commonplace ulterior transactions have generally conceded positive social value in providing important protection for the parties to the transaction while they explore the potential for their future transactions with each other.

However, ulterior transactions are also involved in maladaptive, inauthentic communication, where the REPETITION COMPULSION leads both parties complementarily to set each other up to replay some of their painful childhood experiences. In such cases, the protagonists are far less likely to be conscious of the ulterior transactions they are involved in, and yet much more compulsively driven to use them than when they use them consciously in a socially adaptive way.

Strokes

There is a great deal of evidence that, deprived of sufficient stimulation through skin-to-skin contact, the human infant will degenerate organically (as well as psychically) in much the same way as if deprived of food. For Berne, this truth—for which he acknowledges the findings of René Spitz (who famously discovered that the deaths of healthy infants in a Paris orphanage during World War II were attributable to the lack of physical stroking they were receiving)—led him to postulate the need to be stroked as the primary psychological motivator of all behaviour from the cradle to the grave.

Once the period of close physical intimacy with his mother is over, the individual, for the rest of his life, perpetually strives to recapture the perfect unconditional stroking he once received. But after infancy this is difficult to get—at least often—yet our stroke *needs* are continuous and imperative. So, as Berne (1961) put it in his book, *Transactional Analysis in Psychotherapy*,

> Under most conditions he will compromise. He learns to do with more subtle, even symbolic forms of handling, until the merest nod of recognition may serve the purpose to some extent, although his original craving for physical contact may remain unabated. As the complexities increase, each person becomes more and more individual in his quest, and it is these differences which lend variety to social intercourse. (p. 84)

In TA a stroke is any act implying recognition of another's presence—from the primary physical stroke to its most symbolic derivative, from the intensely valued, 'I love you', to the very slightly valued nod of recognition from a passing acquaintance. Although the primary quest is for the original strokes to the sensual Child, derivatively strokes may be given from and received by any ego state. (Every transaction is a stroke.) A child who is thanked by his mother for looking after his little brother so well while she was out receives a stroke to his Parent from his mother's Parent. A child given a present for being top of her class in maths is given a Parent to Adult stroke. A man telling his girlfriend she is beautiful is giving her a Child to Child stroke.

As well as being intrinsically gratifying to the recipient, strokes also serve to reinforce the behaviour they are given for. Thus the boy who is praised by his mother for looking after his little brother will tend to look after his brother even better the next time he is given the opportunity; the child who came top in maths will work even harder to maintain her position; and the girl praised for her beauty will feel, and hence be, more beautiful in future.

Our continual need—and consequent quest—for strokes, as for food, provides the basic structure to the whole of our lives, and engaging in contact with others is a vital, not optional, requirement for our well-being. Strokes are so vital to us that any stroke—that is, any act of recognition—is better than none. We would rather receive a negative stroke—an angry word, a put-down, a hostile glance—than be ignored and receive no stroke at all. Every parent and teacher is familiar with the child who, being unable to get any positive strokes for being 'good', at least makes sure of getting some negative strokes for being 'bad'.

The inefficacy of *punishment* (negative strokes) in eliminating undesired behaviour has been indisputably demonstrated in the experimental results of B.F. Skinner, the far-reaching conclusions from which are dishearteningly little appreciated in society at large. What a negative stroke does accomplish is to *suppress the undesired behaviour momentarily, while the punishment is being inflicted*; but the behaviour will reassert itself with *increased vigour* (having been stroked, albeit negatively) as soon as the punishment is lifted. This truth is largely unrealised by most people—although animal trainers have always known it.

Which kinds of strokes were the typical currency of our childhoods will largely determine the stroke currency we will transact with for the rest of our lives (just as the kind of food we are given as children will largely determine our tastes for the rest of our lives). Some popular stroke currencies are food, money, power, intelligence, physical attractiveness, prestige and status. *Our stroke currencies define the ways we measure the worth of ourselves and others with our Parent.*

Positive strokes reinforce the behaviour or other TRAITS they are given for *and* make us feel good about ourselves; negative strokes reinforce the behaviour or other TRAITS they are given for *and* make us feel bad about ourselves. Children reared on nourishing food will tend to eat nourishing food throughout their lives and so help to maintain their overall health; children reared on crisps and fizzy drinks will tend to go on consuming them in adult life and, by so doing, will prejudice their overall health. *We are addicted to whatever we are given as children*; and so, sadly, 'the rich tend to get richer and the poor poorer'.

HEALTH AND PATHOLOGY

Structural health and pathology

Structurally, for Transactional Analysis as well as for psycho-analysis, health is defined in terms of the individual's ability to obtain maximum satisfaction for the contents of all the structures of his being. As in psychoanalysis, Transactional Analysis looks for the conflicts in the substance of the whole self that are associated with an individual's dis-ease, and then seeks to resolve these conflicts through modifying maladaptive existential *decisions* and the negative stroke patterns associated with them. But, unlike psychoanalysis, TA understands that maladaptive contents of the psyche can be healed *rapidly* by reference to the conscious and pre-conscious contents of the psyche, which can be easily and quickly accessed, rather than through the prolonged process of accessing repressed—often pre-verbal—contents of the psyche.

Functional health and pathology

The Parent, Adult, and Child ego states in each individual make up the whole of his or her ego. But although everybody's ego is made up of these same basic components, most people have *unequal amounts of energy* in each of their ego states. A perfect balance of ego states is rare in real life; and it would be a dull world if we were all so balanced. We need people with a little extra Parent to be our good doctors and nurses and counsellors and ministers of religion. We need people with a little extra Adult to be our good lawyers and scientists and research workers and computer operators. And we need people with a little extra Child to be our good artists and entertainers and inventors and dress designers.

Healthily, people have *enough* energy invested in each of their ego states that they can respond from the appropriate ego state to the usual situations of everyday life, even though individuals prefer situations and activities that use their own most energised ego states.

But transitory *impasses* between our functioning ego states is also a normal part of everyday life. Sometimes the Parent and Adult are opposed in their perception of a *decision* to be made; or the Parent and Child find it difficult to resolve a conflict between them; or the Adult and Child despair of finding realistic ways to get what the Child wants.

Healthily, such impasses are resolved in a relatively short time. It is when the issues of one or other of these *impasses* become chronic that functional pathology may result. These unresolved impasses may be a new problem that crops up in our lives or an old matter from childhood that continues to affect us, either of which may be *too painful for us to face*. When we reach this point, we are inclined to cheat ourselves into feeling that there really is no problem. We force the battling ego states into a truce by providing them with a *pseudo-solution that keeps both of them quiet*. By this means *we feel better, but actually make things worse*. We achieve this by CONTAMINATING the relevant ego states, which is an essentially dishonest thing to do.

Consider the case of a man whose Parent ego state was taught, 'All Black people are stupid'. (Some parents give their children some pretty nasty Parent values.) But Adult reality faces this man with a highly intelligent Black neighbour—a university professor of Philosophy—whose very great intelligence is an uncomfortable fact. Now the honest thing for our man to do would be to face the discomfort of the disagreement between his Adult and Parent and allow the perceived Adult reality of a very intelligent Black man to amend his Parent ego state. If he did this, he would be likely to form an appropriate judgement such as, 'I was brought up to believe all Black people are stupid. This is clearly not the case, so I no longer have this belief.' But renouncing our beliefs—even in the face of overwhelming facts—requires courage, and most people are more likely to attempt to bend the facts, if necessary, and cling tenaciously to their beliefs, however outdated. Our man with the Parent belief, 'All Black people are stupid', is likely to decide, 'My Black neighbour is very intelligent, but of course he's the exception that proves the rule.' This is prejudice.

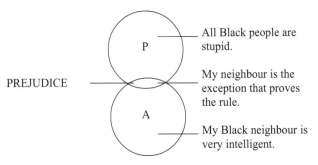

Figure 12   Prejudice

When the Adult and Child are CONTAMINATED we have delusion. Consider the case of a girl whose Child ego state is in love with a man, but the man hardly knows her and certainly is not in love with her (Adult reality). The girl goes to a party where the man she loves is present. He doesn't talk to her all evening. If she cannot bear to face the reality that her feelings are not reciprocated, she may interpret the situation to suit her Child wishes and say to her best friend, the next day, 'He must be in love with me or he wouldn't have ignored me the way he did last night.'

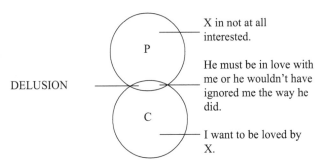

Figure 13   Delusion

When Parent and Child are CONTAMINATED we get confusion. Consider the case of a woman who tries on a dress in a department store. Her Child loves it and wants it but, as her Parent, she should, instead, pay the gas bill. She tries it on and takes it off several times, immobilised by her conflict, with neither ego state willing to concede victory to the other. Finally, believing her Child to have won the battle, she writes out a cheque in payment for the dress and asks to have it sent to her address. Three days later, the department store phones her and apologetically tells her that they cannot deliver the dress until she writes them another cheque, as she has put next year's date on the original one.

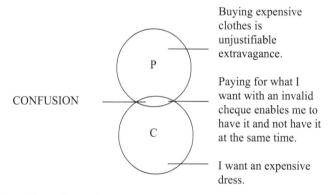

Figure 14   Confusion

In therapy, CONTAMINATIONS are best broken up by the use of the energy of the person's third ego state—the one that is not involved in the CONTAMINATION. Thus the prejudiced man might be challenged with, 'How would you *feel* (Child) if somebody talked about you like that?'; the deluded girl might be challenged with, 'He's not worthy of you (Parent) and there are plenty more fish in the sea'; and the confused woman might be confronted with, 'How about putting a deposit on it and paying for it in instalments?' (Adult).

There is an even more radical resolution for the problem of a chronic *impasse* between ego states than CONTAMINATIONS and that is exclusion. By REPRESSING the attitudes or perceptions of one or two ego states to unconsciousness, *impasses* are denied by complete evasion. Clearly this leads to a greatly impoverished personality and life. There are six different possible forms of exclusion, three exclusions of one ego state and three exclusions of two ego states. The effective exclusion of two ego states from most of an individual's daily life is clearly the most impoverishing defence of all against awareness of impasses, and may require the methods of psychoanalysis for the issues to be brought into awareness and healed.

An excluded Parent leaves a person without the necessary generalised precepts to behave responsibly or in a caring way towards himself or others. Such a person is usually perceived by others to be *uncaring*.

An excluded Child makes a person lack emotional expressiveness and insight. Such a person is usually perceived by others as *joyless*.

An excluded Adult results in a chronic condition of hyper-emotionality. Such a person is usually perceived by others to be *turbulent*.

The *cold person* can be observed in the stereotype of the utterly boring scientist who insists on using his Adult exclusively to deal with all of life in order to avoid facing his unresolved Parent–Child conflicts.

The *harsh or smothering person* is found in the stereotype of the preacher—all Parent—who, metaphorically, refuses to take his dog-collar off—even in bed—rather than bring Adult reality to terms with his Child fantasies. The smothering version is personified in the archetypal Jewish mother of *Portnoy's Complaint* fame.

The *infantile person* is found in the stereotype of the woman who impulsively lives the whole of her life according to the whim of the moment (Child) rather than testing her (usually harsh) Parent against (Adult) reality and extracting some useful generalisations from the dialogue.

RECOMMENDED READING

Berne, E (1961) *Transactional Analysis in Psychotherapy*. New York: Grove Press.

Berne, E (1973) *What Do You Say After You Say Hello?* New York: Bantam.

Klein, Mavis (1981) *How to Choose a Mate.* London: Marion Boyars.

Skinner, BF (1960) *Science and Human Behaviour*. New York: Macmillan.

Steiner, C (1975) *Scripts People Live*. New York: Grove Press.

9

THE PROCESS OF THERAPY

Insofar as the defences of the ego have endeavoured to restrain the id impulse, the psychodynamic therapist comes on the scene as a disturber of the peace. The client seeks therapy because, while his defence mechanisms have done their best, they have not fully succeeded in enabling him to heal his psychic wounds sufficiently to get his present needs and desires met.

All psychodynamic therapies share three assumptions:
1. the reality of unconscious mental processes;
2. TRANSFERENCE; and
3. RESISTANCE.

TRANSFERENCE

Loosely speaking, transference consists of the client's emotional attitude to her analyst. Awareness of the power of 'transference' has been, ever since Freud discovered it (see Chapter 1, p. 12) a key concept in all psychodynamic therapies. Transference is the idea that the present relationship of an individual to people and the world is unconsciously influenced by past relationships. In particular, it is understood that the relationship of the client to his analyst recapitulates her childhood relationship with her parents. In the process of therapy, the client transfers her antagonism and/ or love for significant people in her early environment to the therapist; and the therapist, in turn, reacts to the client with the COUNTER-TRANSFERENCE of his own conflicts and repressed ideas.

While the psychotherapist's feelings are acknowledged in the concept of COUNTER-TRANSFERENCE, the 'rights' of the clients' feelings are, naturally, given priority since she is paying freely to express her feelings, and the therapist is being paid to suppress his feelings to the extent that their expression would interfere with the client's emotional catharsis.

Many orthodox psychoanalysts believe that the analysis of

'the transference' is the cornerstone of the therapeutic process, which can only be achieved by the analyst being a BLANK SCREEN onto which the ANALYSAND PROJECTS his or her feelings. To this extent, an orthodox psychoanalyst either remains altogether out of sight of the client or at least presents and maintains a po-faced neutrality, giving no advice or direct reassurance, but occasionally offering an emotion-free analytical interpretation.

In order for an interpretation to be valid—and thus useful to the client—it must make sense to both analyst and client. A typical phrase by which clients affirm the correctness of an analyst's interpretation is, 'I never thought of it that way before', followed by new material fitting into the emerging pattern of the jigsaw puzzle of the client's psyche.

RESISTANCE

Resistance refers to the opposition encountered during psycho-analytic treatment to the process of making the unconscious conscious. It is the backlash of the defence mechanisms.

When resistance emerges, therapy is clearly under way, but the client is likely to want to terminate the therapy at this time, which he will RATIONALISE and justify in various ways, including, 'This is not really helping me', and, 'It's been useful so far, and I feel much better, so I don't feel the need of continuing.'

This is the point at which the therapist's greatest skills are brought to bear in persuading the client *to trust the therapist's professional judgement*, and that these impulses to leave the therapy are premature. Indeed, from the analyst's point of view, what has been achieved before resistance is encountered has little if any value, if the process is terminated at this time. This is the time when 'counselling' is transformed into *true psychotherapy*. It is the therapist's prime obligation to put herself and her client through the challenge of bearing and overcoming the resistance which, in due course, is profoundly appreciated by the client. And, in anticipatory support of the therapist's task, the client is asked to agree, before the therapeutic relationship begins, to pay for all sessions, irrespective of absence, for any reason. As Woody Allen put it in his film *Annie Hall*, 'If you drop dead of a heart attack, they make you pay for the sessions you miss.'

CURE

Many clients, in their initial consultation with a therapist, ask, 'How long will it take?' While, of course, there is no definitive answer to this question, it is generally the case that deeply transformative work cannot be achieved in less than a year or two of weekly therapy sessions.

In absolute terms, psychological health and pathology are indefinable. Any frame of reference constructed by us out of our early experiences is as legitimate as any other. Pragmatically, however, the attributions 'healthy' or 'pathological' are relative terms based on the extent to which an individual's frames of reference enable him to get his needs met in his relationships with other people and that neither IDENTIFICATION nor PROJECTION plays an important part in those relationships.

From the client's point of view, he embarks on a course of psychotherapy in order *to get rid of his symptoms*. But his symptoms are not his dis-ease, and the therapist is bound to explain to the client that he will only lose his symptoms if (1) he understands their origin; and (2) that his conscious wish to lose his symptoms is greater than his (defence mechanisms') wish to retain the status quo.

VARIETIES OF PSYCHODYNAMIC THERAPY

The most important general feature of newer psychodynamic therapies has been the attempt to reduce the length of the procedure, from years to months, or even to a fixed number of sessions agreed in advance. Ironically, short-term analysis is much closer to what Freud did than the prolonged process that subsequently became de rigueur for orthodox psychoanalysts. This has much to do with the fact that, at first, Freud was unaware of TRANSFERENCE and the curative power of the TRANSFERENCE process, which takes so long. Contemporary schools of psychodynamic therapy differ from each other in the balance they seek to achieve between the advantages and disadvantages of the TRANSFERENCE relationship. For example, orthodox psychoanalysts make the unravelling of the TRANSFERENCE relationship a cornerstone of their therapy; whereas TA therapists (in accordance with Berne's view) typically insist on a rational, equal-to-equal relationship with the client, and are inclined to 'cross' a Child to Parent TRANSFERENCE transaction with an Adult to Adult response.

There is now a vast array of HUMANISTIC therapies for a prospective client to choose amongst. Some strictly avoid touching between client and therapist and so remain true to the 'talking cure' that is psychoanalysis; others value highly the beneficial effects of (literal) stroking; others do both in about equal measure. Therapies involving body work are generally inclined to encourage physical hugs, at least amongst members of therapy groups.

GROUP THERAPY

Most potential clients declare that they want individual, not group, therapy. This desire is rationalised in various ways, including, of course, their desire for undivided attention, as well as their inhibitions about disclosing themselves amongst strangers whom they may dislike or who might otherwise discomfort them. Yet individuality itself is formed in the social context of the family, as are our hang-ups, and the therapy group can provide a quasi-ideal family in which all the shortcomings of our original family are negated. Furthermore, at the confrontational level of therapy, the consensual agreement of members of the group helps the therapist in her task, as well as facing the client with the unassailable truth of the issues he needs to face. Conversely, when there is consensual disagreement with the therapist, the therapist enhances the respect her clients feel for her by her willingness to be mistaken.

Only-children particularly benefit from group therapy, although, of course, they are most resistant to it. Out of their deprivation of the give and take of sibling love, hate, rivalry, aggression, and negotiation, all only-children have some important gaps in their ability to transact well at a Child to Child level. In a group setting, they, more than others, either self-centredly demand all the attention of the therapist or else over-reticently withdraw into silence. The group experience is a particular challenge to them, and can rectify their deficient childhood experience.

There are some clients who are too disturbed to participate in group therapy, which might be thought of as therapy for the three-to-six-year-old in each of the clients. Clients who are extremely depressed or anxious are in need of therapy for the pre-three-year-old in themselves, and individual therapy fulfils that need, granting them undivided maternal-type nourishment that they need before they can rise to the challenge of the eroticised social world.

RECOMMENDED READING

Faraday, A (1975) *The Dream Game*. New York: Penguin.

Freud, S (1967) *The Interpretation of Dreams*. London: George Allen & Unwin.

Foulkes, SH & Anthony, EJ (1957) *Group Psychotherapy*. London: Penguin.

Malcolm, J (1981) *Psychoanalysis: The impossible profession*. London: Picador.

Rycroft, C, Gorer, G, Storr, A, Wren-Lewis, J & Lomas, P (1968) *Psychoanalysis Observed*. London: Penguin.

Yalom, ID (2002) *The Gift of Tears*. London: Piatcus.

10

PSYCHODYNAMIC COUNSELLING
TRANSCRIPTS

THE ADVANTAGES OF GROUP THERAPY

Few therapists would dispute the efficacy of group treatment compared with individual treatment—not to mention the facts that it is cheaper for the client and earns the therapist a better living.

The group is a microcosm of the world, in which the client can play out her PROTOCOL in the presence of insightful but accepting and non-critical witnesses. Man is a strictly group animal, and solitary confinement is always the harshest punishment.

It is through the sharing within a group that an individual can also experience the harmonious reconciliation he so often needs to find between 'being' and 'doing' and 'giving' and 'taking'. Very often people begin therapy with a CONTAMINATION of the concepts of 'giving' and 'taking', evidenced in apologies they are prone to make for 'taking too much of the group's time' in airing and seeking help for their own problems. Implicitly, they tend to divide the length of time of the session exactly by the number of people present and to take only their 'entitlement'. But they learn that very much of their 'taking' is in fact 'giving' to others of themselves, and that, in free and spontaneous transactions with others, the polarities disappear in a blend that is equally gratifying to all the participants.

THE CONDUCT OF THE THERAPIST

While TA therapy, which emphasises the *social* nature of health and pathology, is particularly effective as a group therapy, many TA therapists also see clients for individual sessions. Following are some extracts from a TA group therapy session and an individual session. Every TA therapist is free to function from all of her ego states in accordance with her own style. However, most TA therapists adopt the rules that nearly all psychodynamic therapists agree are the minimum restraints needed for therapy to proceed safely and effectively.

At any moment in any group therapy session an incalculably large number of 'events' are occurring in words and body language and in the minds of all the people present. When therapist and group are in top form, they may be able to make conjoint use of two—or perhaps three—simultaneously occurring different levels of 'happening', but by and large what gets analysed is (for reasons which must be infinitely multifarious and complex) what makes the greatest impact on the therapist's consciousness.

RULES OF CONDUCT FOR GROUP MEMBERS

Here are the rules that this writer asks for agreement on from clients entering group therapy. Apart from Rule 1, which is considered particularly important by nearly all TA therapists (but is rarely demanded by other therapeutic schools), the other rules are commonplace amongst all psychodynamic therapists.

1. Most TA therapists make a *CONTRACT for change* for each group member, which represents the aim(s) of the individual in being in the group, and the achievement of which indicates their readiness to leave the group. A CONTRACT must be formulated in such a way that its accomplishment will be tangibly visible to other group members and the therapist, as well as known to the individual concerned.

2. No sex or violence is allowed in the group (that is, no uncontained id expression).

3. In order to resign from the group, members agree to come to the group and talk over their reasons for wishing to leave before actually deciding to. No resignation is considered in the first six weeks of membership of the group, since it takes at least this time for a new member to appreciate the potential of the group to meet his personal needs.

[This rule is particularly emphasised as a preliminary to any individual being offered a place in a group. It is especially important because, almost universally, everybody, at some time or another during the course of therapy, feels an Adapted Child impulse to flee, when continuing in therapy makes painful new awareness feel inevitable and imminent. So the explicit agreement is required of each individual that, no matter how they feel, they give at least a month's notice of their intention to leave the group, thus giving the therapist and other group members the opportunity to help them over any hurdle of Adapted Child RESISTANCE that may be (often unconsciously) prompting their desire to leave. (It is often at this point that true therapy begins. Of course, some people do break this rule and leave without notice. These people must be counted amongst the therapist's failures, but since the client knows he has broken the rule, he has at least learnt a lesson about the need for himself to accept some responsibility for the changes in his life that he wants.)]

4. Group members pay for every session irrespective of absence for whatever reason. (Discretionary policies in this matter are too hard to manage.)

5. Any transactions which take place between a group member and the therapist outside the group (on the phone or in an individual session) are the 'property' of the group.

EXTRACTS FROM A GROUP THERAPY SESSION

  Present: Four out of six members of the group (Martin, Alan,
    Keith and Richard)
  Time: 7.30–9.30 p.m.

Martin is a twenty-eight-year-old man, the only son in a family of five children. At present he is a semi-self-employed carpenter. His chief manifest problem is that, for him, 'work' and 'pleasure' are incompatible. His CONTRACT is: *To dialogue between his Adult and Parent in order to reconstitute his Parent in the interest of being able to make appropriate judgements about people and situations.*

Keith is a twenty-four-year-old man, an only child. He is engaged to be married and is currently a postgraduate research student in Chemistry. His chief burden is his only-childness, which makes Child to Child transactions very difficult for him. He also feels alienated from his parents' working-classness, but is also hostile to many middle-class values. His CONTRACT is: *To become fluent in authentic Child to Child transactions.*

Alan is a twenty-three-year-old man, the second of three children. He has an older and a younger sister. He graduated from university a couple of years ago, since when he has been in a more or less constant state of non-specific anxiety, sometimes acute. His chief problem derives from his relationship to his mother, who is an (unacknowledged) alcoholic and is emotionally dependent on Alan. His CONTRACT is *(1) to resolve his 'unfinished business' with his mother; and (2) to pay off his overdraft.*

Richard is a twenty-three-year-old man, an only child. His father died when Richard was fourteen. He is burdened (1) by a belief that 'likeableness' and 'success' are incompatible in a man; and (2) his propensity to form 'triangular' relationships with girlfriends whom he doesn't really want. His CONTRACT is *(1) to choose a future career; and (2) to work through his unexpressed grief for his father and his ambivalent feelings towards his mother.*

Therapist: I think, Keith, I ought to make a point—since you're planning to leave the group soon—of making sure every week of expressly drawing you in—especially as you expressed appreciation last week to Richard for doing so … So what are you going to give us tonight?

Keith: I don't know.

Th: Fair enough, but there was a kind of abruptness in the way you said that, as if to freely associate into another thought is somebody else's business to initiate or …

K: I said what I had to say at that point and that was it.

Th: OK. Anyhow, the important thing tonight is that you have already said something.

K: Yeah.

Th: Talking is giving and it doesn't really matter what the content is.

K: I don't necessarily agree.

Th: What do you mean, 'necessarily'?

K: Because I don't necessarily think this kind of dialogue's constructive.

Th: Constructive to what end?

K: To fulfilling my CONTRACT … You're getting very frustrated with me.

Th: (mildly) No, no.

Richard: Well, I'm getting frustrated. [To Keith] You don't want to go any further with the analysis and won't play along with questions you're being asked. It's frustrating watching you.

K: Yeah, that's the feedback that I'm getting.

Th: OK. Perhaps when you relax, later, we'll relax, too, and we'll stop thinking about content and you'll simply be talking.

K: Maybe.

Th: If you're willing …

*****

Th: [To the group as a whole] Alan rang me up very distressed after our last session.

Alan: Yeah. Actually it was what Sally [a member of the group, absent tonight] said that I thought was a big put-down. I think that was more important than the teasing, which I found merely irritating.

Th: Did she remind you of your mother?

A: Yeah, because it was as if she was saying, 'Don't be vulnerable, I don't want to see you vulnerable …'

R: And that her feeling, right or wrong, was that, as a result of that, she wanted to mother you. She was making a comment about her own feelings.

A: She was also venting a bit … I was feeling very vulnerable then … venting something on me.

R: I think she was making a statement about herself, not you. What was there in that to make you upset? What's wrong with feeling vulnerable?

A: Yeah. It's just that sometimes I feel *so* vulnerable that at that point I felt particularly vulnerable for some reason last week … I felt she was saying, 'Whatever you do, don't be vulnerable.' I'm sorry to go off the subject, but I've got sort of … I had palpitations as I was coming here for some reason, and I've only had three hours sleep in the last thirty-six hours.

Th: Why have you had so little sleep?

A: I've been on a long shift [at work].

Th: Were you frightened of coming here tonight?

A: Yeah.

Th: What of?

A: Frightened of revealing myself.

Th: Revealing which part of yourself?

A: Well I had a raw nerve in me struck last week and I felt it wasn't something I wanted to deal with.

Th: Was it a kind of reiteration of your childhood relationship with your sisters, your big sisters, who always discounted you by teasing you?

A: I just … I mean I … Er … You know, I feel in a sense, there's no point in my being here tonight because I'm not prepared to go through with it at the moment and so we're really wasting our time talking about it.

Th: You're not wasting anybody's time. I'm not going to push you if you wholeheartedly don't want to pursue the topic any more. But remember, this is a very protected environment.

A: Yeah.

Th: I think your sensitivity makes you respond to everything with a much more intensity than is warranted. Things other people have forgotten five minutes later, you go around feeling the power of for a whole day.

A: Well, I know, yeah. I mean my sister said that last Friday.

Th: It could be turned to something very adaptive. You have an immense capacity for analytical understanding of situations …

*****

Th: Martin? [who has not yet spoken this evening]
Martin: Mm?
Th: When are you going to tell us what *you're* frightened of?
M: Well I think it's a matter of being vulnerable. It's the thing I most want to express … it's a sort of rejected feeling. Draw me in, I suppose.
Th: How?
M: In the way you've just done. I don't want nurturing. I want taking apart. I mean I can be fairly vulnerable amongst people I'm familiar with, but there's always a shell there.
R: I want to change my job pretty soon and I'd like some ideas, some suggestions. I just really don't know … I once thought I'd like to have a go at telephone sales, but it's very high pressure.
Th: Would you like to be a salesman, generally?
R: No, not generally.
Th: Are you looking for a job now to see you through to a year in September when you start your law course again?
R: Right. Yes. But when I go back to do that one year, I'll have spent as many years in the third year as most people spend doing a whole degree.
Th: But you'll have done a lot else for yourself in the meanwhile as well [meaning personal growth through therapy].
R: I accept that. Has anybody got any ideas?
M: There's a job advertised in Harrow Sports Centre—a Security Assistant, £210 a week.
R: I'm guessing, but probably it's shift work …
M: Yes, it is.
A: What about a job centre, an employment agency,

something like that?

M: There are a lot of people employed in the Building Centre—off Tottenham Court Road. It's a place where you go to find out anything you want to know about building materials. And there's a library there.

R: Actually the Building Centre sounds marvellous, and also the library idea.

Th: You'd like something quite peaceful, then?

R: Yes.

Th: OK then.

[End of session]

EXTRACTS FROM AN INDIVIDUAL SESSION

While group therapy is inevitably more complex than individual therapy, for the beginner therapist it can be easier than one-to-one sessions. While members of a group are transacting with each other, the group therapist is given a chance to withdraw a little to process her thoughts and feelings, whereas in one-to-one sessions she needs to be constantly responsive. Below is an extract from a one-to-one therapy session.

Emma (26) and Giles (33) met about a year ago and are very much in love. They are to be married in about 6 weeks' time. The only bar to their present happiness is the difficulty they have—separately and together—in relating to Emma's mother. They have consulted a counsellor together, for a number of sessions. Emma has requested this session on her own.

Therapist: Okay. Fire away.

Emma: I'm going to visit my mother on my own for a few days to sort things out. I'm very in love with Giles and very much want to marry him. I feel as though I'm completely caught in the middle of my mother and my husband-to-be, which is absolutely ridiculous. I know I have tried to stand up to my Mum, and I sympathise with Giles, but I can't cut my entire family out of my life. But him not giving anything gives her loads of ammunition for kind of, you know, her turning against him, which is ridiculous.

Th: You're in conflict between your literal Parent and your Child, aren't you?

E: Absolutely. I just can't believe she doesn't want our well-being. She doesn't say she doesn't like him, but she says she doesn't think he makes me happy … She objected to my previous boyfriends as well.

Th: What do you want to achieve by your visit to your mother?

E: I'm going there to convey my happiness. That's my mission.

Th: Great.

E: I do understand his point …

Th: Do you understand he's got a good case?

E: I think he's got a bloody good case. But he's put up such a barrier. He won't allow in her good points, and I just can't believe she doesn't want us to be happy. But, you know, there'll always be something, with anyone.

Th: I think he likes it when you have a hard time with your Mum because it gives him the opportunity to let off steam about his own feelings towards her.

E: I can't bear it, especially when nothing happened and we [her mother and herself] had a nice time.

Th: You really mustn't discuss your mother with Giles at all.

E: Absolutely. I'm going there (to visit her mother) with a view to conveying my happiness. And the other reason is I'm going to come back to Giles as a happy person. That's my mission.

Th: What do you think it is she actually does that gets to him?

E: I think it's a control thing in her, which he can't bear because he's a control freak himself. He also says he can't bear how upset I get over anything to do with her.

Th: What are *your* problems with your mother?

E: I do believe she wants my happiness. I mean sometimes I completely dislike her personality, the way she is … the way she talks to people and talks about people and talks over people … You know, she lays the law down. She had a very unhappy childhood. She hated her own mother. She was deserted by her parents and brought up by her grandparents. She had an extremely, unbelievably bad childhood, and I think she lets it all out in her anger.

Th: And she probably wants, in her Parent, to be so much better a parent to you than her parents were to her.

E: Absolutely.

Th: But the problem for your mother—and for all of us—is that our Adapted Childs have so much more power than our Parent ego states. Unconsciously, from her Adapted Child, your mother is being unloving, even though her Parent wants to be the opposite.

E: Yeah.

Th: She needs to be cut off from anything that gives her negative power over you. At a deep level, she is only able to express love when she sees other people having as negative a view of life as she has … so she can say, 'Oh you poor thing, isn't life terrible?' And every time you have a row with Giles, your mother's Adapted Child wins.

E: I know I need to work on being more detached.

Th: Don't be the victim pawn between Giles and your mother any more. You need to make a decision that, from now on, you will absolutely refuse to talk about your mother to Giles. And when you talk to your mother about Giles, you will only say how happy he makes you. If your mother upsets you, come to talk to me or a friend, but *never* to Giles. From now on, you are going to be the one in control.

E: Absolutely. And it will be for the benefit of everyone, including my mother. Now I feel I've got a grip on the whole situation.

Th: Good.

[The session continued …]

RECOMMENDED READING

Berne, E (1961) *Transactional Analysis in Psychotherapy*. New York: Grove Press.

Berne, E (1966) *The Structure and Dynamics of Groups and Organizations*. New York: Grove Press.

Berne, E (1966) *Principles of Group Treatment*. New York: Grove Press.

Perls, FS (1972) *Gestalt Therapy Verbatim*. New York: Bantam.

11

PSYCHODYNAMIC RESEARCH AND APPLICATIONS

Psychologists are of two kinds; the ones who call themselves scientists and devote themselves to looking for facts about people, usually in controlled laboratory conditions, and the ones who call themselves humanists and devote themselves to looking for and analysing the meanings in people's lives, usually in some kind of therapeutic setting. HUMANISTIC psychologists are predisposed to presume that PROJECTION of subjective reality is overwhelmingly more important than objective fact in our experiences of and observations upon life.

Intrinsic problems

Ever since Freud, the besetting sin of HUMANISTIC psychology, in the view of its critics, has been its ability to explain anything *after* it has happened. From this point of view, psychoanalysis is so comprehensively sophisticated as to be capable of making plausible, non-testable hypotheses about anything and everything. If the facts don't fit one interpretation, then another interpretation can be found or some undiscovered facts inferred.

Attempts to break down this hostility to psychoanalytic thought are probably unwise and nearly always fruitless. The convictions of both parties to the argument are important enough to each of them that the pretence that each is being reasonable is likely to exacerbate their mutual hostility while their opposed beliefs remain unmodified by argument, for

A man convinced against his will

Is of the same opinion still. (author unknown)

To the extent that science tests its hypotheses by measurement, psychoanalysis is not science; its truths are of a different order.

Psychodynamic psychology (and other HUMANISTIC

psychologies) is seeking *accuracy,* not *measurable exactitude.* Its truths are commonly referred to as 'authenticity', as are the truths of music, literature, painting and poetry, our direct experiences of love and hate, responsibility and guilt, pride and shame and tragedy … in short, all things human. Human truths are QUALITATIVE truths concerning meaning, and are irrefutably validated by their oft-repeated affirmation in the subjective experiences of many people. Thus, much 'scientific' research into the validity and/or efficacy of *psychoanalysis* is of sophisticated QUANTITATIVE methods applied to partial and/or trivial components of theory or therapy.

Ironically, Freud constantly claimed to be scientific, in accordance with his desire for his theory to be intellectually respectable; in his time, even more than in ours, the scientific paradigm was *the* truth. But, actually, psychoanalysis is much more akin to philosophy than science; Freud was *speculating,* and there is no more chance of 'proving' the truth of his ideas than there is of 'proving' Plato's Theory of Forms. Nevertheless, in today's world, where competition is tough for money and favours, many psychodynamic theories find themselves bowing to the demand to (scientifically) prove their validity and efficacy in measurable ways, which has been achieved to a limited extent.

Testing the efficacy of psychoanalytic therapy

Freud developed the clinical procedure of psychoanalysis from:

1. the interpretation of RESISTANCE and TRANSFERENCE;
2. the understanding of adult behaviour in terms of childhood experiences; and
3. the analysis of symptoms as adaptive strategies.

Through these ideas and procedures, psychoanalytic therapy aims to enable the individual to become acquainted with his or her unconscious feelings and impulses, and, in new freedom, release imprisoned emotion, and give up illusions that once served a purpose but now bring only unhappiness. Making these discoveries increases the individual's sense of personal responsibility, releasing him from being helplessly at the mercy of the emotional influences of the past in favour of gaining a wider choice of action.

It seems probable that there are two main factors that both promote and indicate an individual's recovery from NEUROTIC distress:

1. the client adopts some scheme or system of thought which appears to him to make sense of his distress; and
2. he or she makes a relationship of a fruitful kind with another person.

Common sense would suggest that simply asking clients how much of these two factors they have gained through psychotherapy would be the most valid way to test its efficacy; but clients' reportage, at least during therapy, will be highly coloured by *positive* or *negative* TRANSFERENCE (which may continue well after termination of the therapy unless that termination is an ideal one).

Direct evidence

Despite the discountable 'evidence' of so-called research, speciously designed to pour scorn on psychodynamic theories and therapies, there is a body of research undertaken by those with expert knowledge of clinical issues and appropriate research methods. Controlled comparative studies indicate that a high percentage of clients who go through *any* form of psychotherapy do gain from it. About 80 per cent of studies show positive results and conclude that, in general, psychotherapy works, and its effects are not entirely due to non-specific effects, such as arousal of hope, nor to spontaneous recovery. (Could this be because all forms of psychotherapy involve *listening* to the client?)

When comparisons have been made between different psychotherapies, most studies have failed to show significant differences in the success rate between them, although COGNITIVE-based ('problem-solving') approaches do seem to produce higher than average positive outcomes.

Indirect evidence

One of the strongest arguments in favour of psychoanalysis is that it considers man as a biological phenomenon; and ecological research is lately tending to confirm some of its basic hypotheses.

APPLICATIONS

For about the past 80 years, psychoanalytic concepts have so permeated the Western ZEITGEIST as to be woven into the very fabric of our cultural assumptions. From the novels of F. Scott Fitzgerald (writing in the 1930s) to Philip Roth (writing today), and in countless cinematic and theatrical stories up to the contemporary films of Woody Allen, psychoanalysis as theory and therapy has been made explicit. Less overtly, it is embedded in marketing and advertising and in the multitudinous 'personal growth' workshops now considered de rigueur for employees in the middle to upper echelons of corporate life. Freud's heritage is a big part of the atmosphere we all breathe.

RECOMMENDED READING

Donald J (1990) Affect in psychodynamic psychotherapy. *American Journal of Psychotherapy, 44* (2): 274–82.

Greenberg, LS & Pinsof W (eds) (1986) *The Psychotherapeutic Process: A research handbook.* New York: The Guilford Press.

Wolman, BB (1972) *Success and Failure in Psychoanalysis and Psychotherapy.* New York: Macmillan.

Zerbe, KJ (1990) Through the storm: Psychoanalytic theory in the psychotherapy of the anxiety disorders. *Bulletin of the Menninger Clinic, 54* (2): 171–83.

APPENDIX

RESOURCES FOR LEARNING

The beautifully refurbished **Swiss Cottage Library** in London declares its specialist commitment to books on psychoanalysis with the statue of Freud in its grounds. The address is 88 Avenue Road, London NW3 3HA. Phone 020 7974 6522.

MIND—The National Association for Mental Health is a leading charity, with 200 local associations throughout England and Wales, and is a central source of information on all matters pertaining to available therapies and training. Their head office is at 15–19 Broadway, London E15 4BQ. Phone 020 8519 2122.

Many of the organisations listed below have regular lectures and forums open to the public, as well as offering training courses and holding lists of qualified therapists in their specialties.

The British Association of Psychotherapists (BAP) is a leading UK national association for various forms of psychoanalytic training and therapy. Contact them at 37 Mapesbury Road, London NW2 4HJ. Phone 020 8452 9823.

The Institute of Psychoanalysis, 112a Shirland Road, London W9 2EQ. Phone 020 7563 5000.

The Society of Analytical (Jungian) Psychology, 1 Daleham Gardens, London NW3 5BY. Phone 020 7419 8895.

The Adlerian Society (UK) & the Institute for Individual Psychology offer many events open to the public. Contact them at 73 South Ealing Road, London W5 4QR. Phone 020 8567 8360.

Institute of Transactional Analysis, PO Box 1101, Wigton, Cumbria CA7 9YH. Phone 0845 0099101.

Institute of Group Analysis, 1 Daleham Gardens, London NW3 5BY. Phone 020 7431 2693.

The Gestalt Centre, 62 Paul Street, London EC2A 4NA. Phone 020 7613 4480.

The Manchester Gestalt Centre, 7 Norman Road, Manchester M14 5LF. Phone 0161 251 2202.

GLOSSARY

(All glossary entries are shown in SMALL CAPITALS throughout the text, as are cross-references within the glossary.)

ANALYSAND   Term for the client in classical psychoanalysis.

ARCHETYPES   The symbolic contents of the COLLECTIVE UNCONSCIOUS.

BEHAVIOURISM   A 'school' of objective psychology and philosophy which rejects subjective experience and consciousness. It states that the only relevant, valid psychological events are those which can be observed, i.e. behaviour.

BLANK SCREEN   In orthodox psychoanalysis, the analyst is a silent (except for occasional interpretations) BLANK SCREEN on which the analysand projects their psyche.

BOUND (ENERGY)   Energy which remains invested in an earlier stage of development and is locked in place. Such bound energy is called a FIXATION.

CHARACTER   Those aspects of self arising from the imposition of a moral code in the child between the ages of 3 and 6 (the stage of superego development). In TA, the contents and behaviour of the Parent ego state.

COGNITIVE (COGNITION)   Knowing-related thought processes, as opposed to feeling-related or emotional processes.

COGNITIVE (COUNSELLING/BEHAVIOUR THERAPY)   A 'school' of counselling/therapy based on theories which derive from cognitive theory, i.e. place prime importance on rational thought processes.

COLLECTIVE UNCONSCIOUS   Term coined by CG Jung to refer to the part of the unconscious mind inherited culturally.

CONSTITUTION (-AL FACTORS)   Fundamental characteristics and dispositions 'given' at birth either by genetics or because of conditions in utero.

CONTRACT   An agreement between the helper and the client which determines the type of helping relationship it will be and, in TA therapy, the goals the client has set themselves.

CONTAMINATION   A maladaptive, pseudo-resolution of an impasse between ego states in which the incompatible impulses or attitudes of the relevant ego states are expressed in a single, inauthentic idea. See index entries for confusion, delusion and prejudice.

COUNTER-TRANSFERENCE   The emotional response of the counsellor to a client in psychodynamic therapy.

DEATH INSTINCT   See THANATOS

DENIAL   A primitive defence mechanism in which unpalatable aspects of the psychic, personal, social or physical world are denied access to consciousness.

DRIVE   In psychodynamic theory an energetic INSTINCTUAL impulse. In general psychology the hypothetical energy which derives from a physiological state, e.g. the need for food or need for sex.

EGO IDEAL   The part of the superego associated with the individual's conception of how she wishes to be.

EGO PSYCHOLOGY   Psychodynamic theories which emphasise understanding personality and character in terms of the social realities of the ego rather than the (wholly unconscious) fantasies of the id and superego.

FIXATION   The process whereby energy is BOUND at an earlier level of personality or character development through the incomplete resolution of issues associated with that stage of development.

FREE ASSOCIATION   The mode of thinking encouraged in psychoanalytic therapy in which the client spontaneously expresses all his thoughts and feelings as they arise.

HOLOGRAM   A 3-D photograph-like image which if broken or cut into pieces can project the whole image from any of the fragments.

HOMOEOSTASIS   A regulatory mechanism to keep physiological systems in balance. Equilibrium maintained by feedback, e.g. increased body temperature causes sweating which cools down the body and stops sweating reflex. Is also used to explain behaviour via DRIVE-reduction. Body needs food which leads to hunger, eating and balance restored.

HUMANISTIC PSYCHOLOGY   Psychology which perceives people in their wholeness rather than as a collection of discrete mechanisms which can be manipulated.

IDENTIFICATION   A primitive defence mechanism in which an individual avoids hostility towards another by perceiving himself to be the same as the other in important respects.

INSTINCT   An innate, biologically determined DRIVE to action, e.g. the instinct to live.

INTERVENTION   Used to mean counsellor/therapist response or action.

LIBIDO   The overall reservoir of psychic energy directed towards the fulfilment of the PLEASURE PRINCIPLE. Also variously referred to in literature as 'life energy' and 'sexual energy'.

MATURATION   In psychology a natural process of growth and development not contingent on learning, e.g. walking.

MOTIVATION   The (hypothetical) aim of behaviour, i.e. answers the question '*why* do animals behave?'

NARCISSISTIC   When an excessive portion of the ego is directed to self-love (rather than the love of others).

NEUROSIS/NEUROTIC   An emotional disorder which is capable of explanation in terms of maladaptively resolved conflicts in the psyche.

OBJECT RELATIONS   The idea that the ego-self exists only in relation to other objects, which may be external or internal. Also the study of the relationship the individual forms (primarily from early interactions with the parents) to objects and people external to his/her psyche.

OBSESSIVE-COMPULSIVE (DISORDER)   A psychiatric 'illness' where the person ruminates — has repetitive, distressing, intrusive (obsessive) thoughts and associated tasks, ritualised repetitive behaviours (compulsions) in an attempt to alleviate the ruminative thoughts.

ORGANIC CONDITION/DISEASE   A condition or illness with a physical/biological cause (rather than psychological), e.g. brain tumours are physical (organic) entities but symptoms can in some circumstances look like the symptoms of psychological distress (mood swings).

PHOBIA   Irrational fear, taken to a level which interferes with everyday life, such as fear of spiders or moths.

PLEASURE PRINCIPLE   The basic quest of the psyche to experience pleasure and avoid pain.

PRIMARY PREVENTION RESEARCH   Looking at the factors which predispose people to certain conditions/distress, such as social and environmental conditions, and personal characteristics and experiences.

PRIMARY PROCESS   Unconscious mental activity.

PROJECTION   A defence mechanism in which an individual blames another person for his or her own inadequacy.

PROTOCOL   Psychoanalytic term for the life plan laid down by the individual based on his/her experiences in the first six years of life.

PSYCHOSIS   In psychodynamic theory, disturbances in which the individual has lost the ability to function in terms of the REALITY PRINCIPLE. Also a medical-model classification of severe distress characterised by loss of contact with reality and lack of insight (person doesn't think they are 'ill'). Includes SCHIZOPHRENIA, clinical depression, bipolar disorder.

QUALITATIVE (CONCEPT)   An idea relating to a quality that cannot be measured precisely. For example, a *red* ball, a *happy* occasion, a *frightening* experience.

QUANTITATIVE (CONCEPT)   An idea relating to a quality that can be measured precisely. For example, *six inches* of rain, a temperature of *ninety-two degrees*.

RATIONALISATION (and justification)   Defence mechanisms in which the individual finds reasons or moral precepts outside himself to account for his thoughts and actions.

REALITY PRINCIPLE   Mental functioning learned through experience of the external world.

REPETITION COMPULSION   The innate tendency to repeat the experiences of infancy and early childhood throughout the rest of life.

REPRESSION   The most radical defence mechanism, in which an unacceptable impulse or idea is made unconscious.

RESISTANCE   The opposition an individual exhibits in psychodynamic therapy to the process of making unconscious processes conscious or to any disturbance in the equilibrium of her/his defence mechanisms.

SCHIZOPHRENIA   Serious psychological distress or mental 'illness'. Classified in medical model as 'PSYCHOSIS'. Many very distressing symptoms of confused, chaotic thoughts and feelings, delusions and hallucinations.

SECONDARY PROCESS   Conscious thinking.

SELF-ACTUALISATION   Term used by many HUMANISTIC psychologists. In the case of Maslow, means the *complete fulfilment of the individual* when all physiological, safety, social and self-esteem needs have been fulfilled.

SEXUAL INSTINCT   The fundamental energy of LIBIDO.

SOCIALISATION   The process by which an individual becomes inducted into society, learning the 'rules and regulations' of living in association with others, from how to conduct yourself in interpersonal relationships to obeying the laws of society.

SPLITTING/EGO SPLITTING   The process in which aspects of the ego are divided into 'good' and 'bad'. The self is identified with the 'good' parts, while the 'bad' parts are relegated to unconsciousness and/or projected on to other people.

SUBLIMATION   A defence mechanism in which LIBIDO is deflected into socially acceptable, non-sexual aims.

SYMBIOSIS/SYMBIOTIC   A mutually beneficial relationship.

SYMBOLISATION   Bringing an experience into conscious awareness and giving it meaning. So pre-symbolic experience would be an experience which either is not yet in awareness and or has no fully developed meaning.

THANATOS   The DEATH INSTINCT, that is the counterpart of LIBIDO, the life instinct.

THERMODYNAMIC MODEL   A psychological model of the structure of the psyche which assumes the fluctuating distribution of a fixed amount of energy.

TRAITS   Inferred (not directly observable) components of personality, an aspect of character such as 'dependability' or 'persistence'. Types (see TYPOLOGY) are collections of traits put together to become 'sorts' of character or personality.

TRANSFERENCE   The process in which a client ascribes thoughts and feelings to the analyst which *actually* refer to previous important figures (usually parents) in the client's life.

TYPOLOGY   A system for classifying things according to their characteristics, particularly a psychological theory which categorises people according to differences of personality between individuals.

UNIFIED FIELD THEORY   The (as yet unrealised) attempt in contemporary physics to find a *single* theory that describes *all* the disparate forces of nature.

UNPLEASURE   Pain.

ZEITGEIST   Literally means 'Spirit of the times': the cultural, social, spiritual, political 'climate' of an era.

INDEX

abandonment 38, 50
Abraham, K 60, 61, 62, 72
accuracy (in measurement) 11, 110
Adapted Child 72, 73, 75, 100, 107
Adler, A 58–9, 65–6
adolescence 43–55, 74
Adult (ego state) 69, 71–6, 77, 79,
  86, 88–9, 91, 92
adult life 37, 52, 55, 57–8
aggression 18, 25, 27, 44–6, 50–1,
  58, 60, 62, 96
anal/anus 18, 36
  FIXATION 32, 42
  stage 32, 36, 39, 42, 45
ANALYSAND 12, 94, 115
Analytical Psychology 60, 66–7,
  113
anima 60, 67
animus 60, 67
Anthony, EJ 97
anxiety 26–7, 29, 33–6, 101 (see
  also 'separation anxiety')
ARCHETYPES 59, 60, 115
attachment theory 62
authenticity 68, 110
authority 24–5
  figures 37
  inner 24
  moral 24
autonomy 44, 51–2, 68

basic needs 24, 31, 37
BEHAVIOURISM 56, 71, 115
bereavement 2, 6
Berne, E 63, 66, 69, 70, 71, 85,
  86, 92
bioenergetics 66, 67
BOUND ENERGY 22, 32–3, 39, 115
Bowlby, J 46, 62–3, 68
breast 15, 32
  bad 60
  good 60

Brenner, C 30
Bromley, DB 55
Burdett, J 5

CHARACTER 7, 19–20, 36–47, 55,
  59, 71, 74, 115
  development 19, 42–6, 55, 59
Chetwynd, T 30
Child (ego state) 69, 71–2, 74–5,
  77, 79, 86, 88–9, 91–2
childhood 7, 8, 12, 20–21, 57, 61,
  64, 85, 89, 93, 97, 110
COGNITIVE/COGNITION 59, 111, 115
COLLECTIVE UNCONSCIOUS 59, 115
competitiveness 59
conduct of the therapist 98–9
conflict 2, 6, 18, 24, 35, 36, 60,
  64, 66, 67, 69, 88–93
confusion 90–1
conscience 16, 24, 26, 40, 43, 45,
  50
conscious 19–20, 24, 26, 50, 59,
  75, 77, 88, 94–5
CONTAMINATION 90–1, 98, 115
CONTRACT for change in therapy
  99, 115
counselling (defining) 1
COUNTER-TRANSFERENCE 93, 116
cultural
  artefacts 29
  conditions 62

Davies, N 5
DEATH 7, 10–11, 15–16, 18, 28, 31,
  42, 48–50, 59–61
  INSTINCT (see 'THANATOS')
defence mechanisms 19, 26–30,
  34, 61, 70, 94
delusion 90
DENIAL 27–8, 30, 36, 43, 50, 116
depression 3, 48, 60, 97, 117
diagnosis 3, 64, 75

displacement 28–9
Donald J 112
dream(s) 11–12, 28, 30, 42, 65
    analysis (Jungian) 65
DRIVE 17–19, 38, 60, 116

EGO 13, 16, 19–20, 23, 25–7, 31,
        33–4, 36–7, 41, 45, 50, 57,
        69, 71, 75, 93
    IDEAL 24, 29, 40, 51, 116
    PSYCHOLOGY 13, 61, 69, 116
    SPLITTING, 62, 118
    states 69, 76 (see also 'Parent',
        'Adult', 'Child')
Electra complex 42
emotional literacy 46
Erikson, EH 46, 55
eros 61 (see also 'LIBIDO')
evidence (in research) 111
    direct 111
    indirect 111
exclusion 91–92
extraversion 59

Fairbairn, WRD 62, 68
Faraday, A 97
FIXATION 31–3, 39, 42, 46, 115
Foulkes, SH 97
Frankl, VE 35
Free Child (ego state) 72–3, 75
Freeman, L 14
Freud, A 10, 13, 30, 46, 61, 68
Freud, S 10, 11,12, 13, 14, 15, 17,
        18, 20, 21, 23, 27, 30, 42,
        46, 48, 49, 56, 57, 58, 59,
        60, 64, 66, 67, 68, 70, 93,
        95, 97, 109, 110, 112, 113
Freud, L 10
Freud Museum 10
Fromm, E 62, 68

gender stereotypical behaviours 48
genital(s) 17–18, 36, 52
    (adult) life 52, 55
    sexual impulses 17, 51
    stage 36, 42, 47

Gestalt therapy 65–7
good enough mother 62
Gorer, G 97
Greenberg, LS 112
group therapy 96–8
growth 23, 31, 36
    personal 5, 112

Hall, CS 21, 68
health 24, 31–5, 40, 43, 52, 60, 64,
        88–92
heterosexual impulse 47
hierarchy of needs 63
HOLOGRAMS 57, 116
HOMOEOSTASIS 15, 116
homosexuality 44
Horney, K 61, 68
HUMANISTIC PSYCHOLOGY 7, 14, 57,
        64, 96, 109–10, 116

id 13, 16, 19–20 22–3, 25, 31, 33,
        37, 41, 42, 70, 71, 75, 93
IDENTIFICATION 18, 27, 44, 47, 52,
        95, 116
impasse 89, 91–2
incestuous desire/impulse 26, 53–4
Individual Psychology 58–9, 66,
        113
INSTINCT 17–8, 22, 24, 26, 28–31,
        34–5, 37, 40, 116
    death (see 'THANATOS')
    maternal 37, 97
    sexual 17, 58
International Transactional
        Analysis Association (ITAA)
        71
interpretation 11, 28, 64–5, 67, 94,
        109–10
intimacy 46, 55, 86
introversion 60

Jones, E 14
Jung, CG 55, 58, 59–60, 62, 67
Jungian analysis 65
justification 29, 40, 45
Klein, Mavis 1, 55, 92

Klein, Melanie 60, 64, 68
latency 46–55, 73
LIBIDO 17, 26, 29, 30, 32, 36, 39,
        47–8, 51, 61, 116
Little Professor 72–3, 75
Lomas, P 97
Lowen, A 66

Malcolm, J 97
Maslow, A 63, 68
maternal instinct 37, 97
MATURATION 23, 36, 47, 54–5, 117
McGuire, W 68
measurement (in research) 109
metaphors 65
moral/ity 51
    authority 24
    standards 54
Moreno, J 66
mouth 17, 36, 38, 39
mysticism 59

Natural Child 72–3, 75
nature 7, 20–1, 36 (see also
        'nurture')
NEUROSIS 11, 27, 33–5, 117
NEUROTIC 10, 40, 42, 49, 62, 111
    anxiety 34
    inhibitions 40, 41
newborn babies 16, 37
Nietzsche 11
Nordby, VJ 68
nurture 7, 20–1

OBJECT RELATIONS 60–2, 117
Oedipal 32, 36, 42–7, 51–2
    battle 43, 53
    FIXATION 32, 46
    stage 32, 36, 44–7, 51, 53, 61, 74
    complex 42, 46
operant conditioning 70
oral 32, 36–7, 39, 47, 60–1
    FIXATION 32, 39
    stage 36
        -biting 38
        -sucking 37

ORGANIC 33
    CONDITION 4, 117
orgasm 15, 37

Parent (ego state) 69, 71, 73–5, 77,
        79, 86, 88–9, 91–2
parental
    control 51
    values 54
pathology 4, 15, 31–5, 59, 61, 63–4,
        88–92, 95, 98
Perls, F 67, 108
personality 36
    development 37–42
PHOBIA 34, 61, 117
Pinsof W 112
PLEASURE 22
    PRINCIPLE 15–16, 22–3, 31, 117
pre-conscious 19–20, 59, 70
prejudice 89–90
PRIMARY
    PREVENTION RESEARCH 4, 117
    PROCESS 23, 38, 49, 117
problem-solving 2, 59, 67, 111
profession 1
PROJECTION 12, 27–9, 95, 109, 117
psychoanalysis 10, 12–15, 19, 32,
        69–70, 74, 88, 92, 109–10
    orthodox Freudian, 36, 64, 93,
        94
psychodrama 66, 67
psychopathic personality 37
PSYCHOSIS 27, 33–4, 117
puberty 17–18, 47 50–5
punishment 17, 25–7, 40–1, 70, 87

rational dialogue 65
RATIONALISATION 13, 29, 94, 96, 118
reaction-formation 29
REALITY PRINCIPLE 16, 23–4, 31, 34,
        38, 41, 47, 49, 53, 118
regression 33
Reich, W 66
REPETITION COMPULSION 19, 46, 55,
        70, 85, 118

REPRESSION 25, 35, 40–1, 50, 52, 58, 62, 70, 118
research 4, 7, 88, 109–12
RESISTANCE 6, 19, 93–4, 100, 110, 118
revelation 6, 64
Riviere, J 68
rules of conduct for therapy group members 99
Rycroft, C 35, 97

satisfaction 15, 17, 22–4, 31–2, 36–7, 88
science 7, 11, 29, 109–10
SECONDARY PROCESS 23, 38, 118
SELF 26
   -ACTUALISATION 63, 118
   -centredness 25, 75, 97
   -discipline 45
   -esteem 26, 42–3, 52–3, 58
separation anxiety 38
sex 3, 15, 18, 25, 27, 99
sexual 17, 50, 51
   desire 46
   development 12
   impulses 12, 44, 51
   instinct (see 'LIBIDO')
   love 48
   self-esteem 43
sexuality 18, 28, 47, 52, 59
shame 25, 49, 110
Sheehy, G 55
short-term analysis 95
Skinner, BF 71, 87, 92
Small, M 14
Spitz, R 85
SPLITTING/EGO-SPLITTING 62, 118
Steiner, C 92
Storr, A 97
stress 2, 6
strokes 67, 70, 79–88
   negative 70, 87
   positive 87
structure of the mind 20, 22–30
SUBLIMATION 24, 29, 30, 118

superego 13, 16, 19–20, 24–6, 31, 33, 37, 40, 44, 50–1, 69, 71, 75
suppression 26, 47
Swiss Cottage Library 113
symbols 59, 65, 86

tenderness 18, 45–6
tension 17, 22, 26, 33, 38
   psychological 12, 15, 33, 38
THANATOS 60–1, 119
THERMODYNAMIC MODEL 15, 119
toilet training 32, 45
Transactional Analysis (TA) 14, 35, 63, 66, 68, 69–92, 96, 98–9
transactions 79–80
   complementary 80–1
   crossed 80–3
   ulterior transactions 80, 84–5
      angular 83, 84
      duplex 84
TRANSFERENCE 12, 93, 110–11, 119
   relationship 12, 64
transitional object 62
trauma 3, 33, 48
tripartite division of the mind 16

unconditional, self-denying love 37
unconscious 13, 19–20, 59
   mind 57
UNPLEASURE 16, 37, 119

Winnicott, DW 62, 68
wish fulfilment 22
Wolman, BB 112
Wren-Lewis, J 97

Yalom, ID 97

ZEITGEIST 15, 60, 112, 119
Zerbe, KJ 112